Crypto Foundations

Demystifying Cryptocurrencies: Your Path to Financial Empowerment

Ariel Thompson

Table of Contents

INTRODUCTION

Welcome to "Crypto Foundations: Demystifying Cryptocurrencies - Your Path to Financial Empowerment." In this e-book, we set out on a quest to solve the mysteries around cryptocurrencies to give you a thorough grasp of this groundbreaking financial phenomenon.

Cryptocurrencies have revolutionized the world of money by creating a decentralized, secure, and borderless method of conducting financial transactions. These digital assets, which were created due to the brilliance of blockchain technology, have disrupted established financial systems and attracted the interest of businesspeople, investors, and ordinary individuals.

This e-book aims to give you the information and assurance you need to navigate the cryptocurrency landscape properly. This e-book will meet your needs whether you are a total novice looking for fundamental clarification or a seasoned investor looking to improve your techniques.

We start our voyage by investigating the background and inception of cryptocurrencies, tracing their development from a purely theoretical notion to a major worldwide financial power. Understanding the history of cryptocurrencies can help to put their influence on the current financial landscape in perspective.

The fundamental workings of cryptocurrencies are then covered, along with an explanation of the intricate ideas behind blockchain technology and cryptography. If you have a firm knowledge of these key elements, you will be well-equipped to understand the inner workings of various cryptocurrencies and their underlying networks.

As we continue on our adventure, we look at some of the most well-known cryptocurrencies on the market, including the innovative Bitcoin, the adaptable Ethereum, and other notable digital assets. You may learn a lot about the wide range of cryptocurrencies by examining their distinctive features and use cases.

With knowledge comes opportunity, and we direct you in your investment endeavors. A good investment strategy must start with understanding market volatility, risk assessment, and selecting the best cryptocurrency exchange. We also examine various cryptocurrency trading strategies to assist you in making educated decisions.

When working with digital assets, security is crucial, thus we dedicate a section to enlightening you on the different cryptocurrency wallet solutions and best practices for shielding your holdings from potential dangers. Additionally, we cover the essential subject of cryptocurrency legislation and legal issues. We want to ensure you understand how this new landscape will affect your cryptocurrency journey as governments and regulatory organizations manage it.

We highlight the numerous uses of cryptocurrencies and blockchain technology across businesses, going beyond investing and trading. We show how cryptocurrencies boost many industries and communities, from social impact and financial inclusion to e-commerce and supply chain management.

There will be difficulties and uncertainties, just like with any innovative technology. We address cryptocurrencies' challenges and preview their potential in the final section. You will better handle the constantly changing world of cryptocurrencies if you know the challenges and opportunities.

Now, set off on this intellectual journey with an eagerness to learn and an open mind. This e-book will equip you to take advantage of cryptocurrencies' enormous potential, whether you are a curious learner or an aspiring crypto enthusiast. Together, let's realize the promise of this financial revolution and open the door to your financial independence.

CHAPTER I

Getting to Know Cryptocurrency

What is Cryptocurrency?

Cryptocurrencies have rapidly emerged as a groundbreaking financial innovation, revolutionizing how we perceive and conduct transactions. Over the past decade, these digital currencies have gained significant traction and disrupted traditional financial systems worldwide. In this section, we will explore the concept of cryptocurrency, its origins, underlying technology, and its transformative impact on the global economy.

A type of digital or virtual currency that employs encryption for safe and decentralized transactions is known as cryptocurrency. Unlike traditional fiat currencies issued and regulated by central authorities like governments and banks, cryptocurrencies operate on decentralized networks known as blockchains. This decentralized nature ensures transparency, security, and immunity from government manipulation.

One of the defining characteristics of cryptocurrencies is their limited supply. Most cryptocurrencies have a predetermined maximum supply, which means they cannot be arbitrarily inflated, leading to a safeguard against inflation. Moreover, transactions with cryptocurrencies are generally irreversible, adding another layer of security and reducing the risk of chargebacks and fraud.

Although the idea of virtual currency has been around since the 1980s, it wasn't until 2009 that the first cryptocurrency, Bitcoin, was released by an unidentified person or group operating under the alias Satoshi Nakamoto. Bitcoin's whitepaper laid the foundation for a decentralized peer-to-peer electronic cash system, introducing the blockchain technology that underpins all cryptocurrencies.

Bitcoin's revolutionary design and the innovative use of blockchain technology sparked interest and curiosity among tech enthusiasts and economists alike. As the first decentralized digital currency, Bitcoin catalyzed the emergence of numerous other cryptocurrencies, collectively known as altcoins, each with unique features and use cases.

The blockchain is central to the operation of cryptocurrencies, a distributed and immutable ledger that records all transactions. The blockchain is made up of several blocks, each of which contains a list of confirmed transactions. A consensus mechanism, which includes proof-of-work or proof-of-stake, is used to add new blocks to the chain, maintaining the integrity and security of the network.

Every member (node) in a blockchain network keeps a copy of the full ledger, doing away with the need for a central authority to monitor and validate transactions. This decentralized approach makes the blockchain resistant to hacking and manipulation, making it an ideal infrastructure for cryptocurrency transactions.

Although Bitcoin is still the most widely recognized and extensively used cryptocurrency, there are many others with unique features and uses. Ethereum, for instance, introduced smart contracts, allowing developers to create decentralized applications (DApps) and deploy programmable code on the blockchain. Ripple (XRP) focuses on enabling fast and low-cost cross-border transactions for financial institutions.

Other cryptocurrencies like Litecoin, Bitcoin Cash, and Cardano have unique attributes catering to specific needs in the digital economy. These cryptocurrencies have found applications in online transactions, remittances, decentralized finance (DeFi), and non-fungible tokens (NFTs), among other use cases.

The advent of cryptocurrencies has had far-reaching implications for the global economy, both positive and negative. The positive effect of cryptocurrencies is that they promote financial inclusion, particularly in areas with little access to conventional banking institutions. Additionally, they enable fast and low-cost cross-border transactions, reducing the reliance on intermediaries like banks and remittance services.

Furthermore, cryptocurrencies have sparked a wave of innovation and investment in blockchain technology, paving the way for new decentralized applications and systems. Projects in DeFi, NFTs, and tokenization of real-world assets are reshaping traditional finance and asset ownership paradigms.

However, cryptocurrencies have also faced criticism and challenges. Volatility remains a significant concern, with rapid price fluctuations leading to speculative trading and investment risks. Additionally, the pseudonymous character of the transactions has sparked concerns about illegal activities including tax evasion and money laundering.

As cryptocurrencies gained popularity, governments and regulatory bodies worldwide grappled with the need to establish appropriate frameworks to govern their use. Some countries have embraced cryptocurrencies, implementing regulations to protect investors and ensure market stability. Others have taken a more cautious approach, raising concerns about consumer protection and financial stability.

The future of cryptocurrencies remains uncertain but promising. As blockchain technology evolves and becomes more scalable and energy-efficient, cryptocurrencies will likely find broader acceptance and integration into various sectors of the economy. Additionally, ongoing research and development may lead to enhanced privacy features, further addressing concerns about illicit use.

In conclusion, cryptocurrencies have transformed the global financial landscape, offering decentralized, secure, and borderless alternatives to traditional fiat currencies. With the birth of Bitcoin and the advent of blockchain technology, a new era of financial empowerment and innovation was ushered in. As cryptocurrencies evolve, their impact on the global economy and society will likely be profound, paving the way for a more decentralized and digitally inclusive future. However, careful consideration of the challenges and responsible regulation will be essential to harness the full potential of this revolutionary technology for the benefit of all.

Importance of Understanding Cryptocurrencies

In the last decade, cryptocurrencies have emerged as a disruptive force, challenging traditional financial systems and captivating the imagination of individuals, investors, and businesses worldwide. While the concept of digital currencies may initially seem daunting, the importance of understanding cryptocurrencies cannot be overstated. This section will explore the significance of comprehending cryptocurrencies, including their potential for financial empowerment, impact on the global economy, and implications for personal and financial security.

Understanding cryptocurrencies empowers individuals to take control of their financial destinies. Unlike traditional financial systems, which are heavily centralized and controlled by banks and governments, cryptocurrencies offer decentralization and financial sovereignty. Knowledge of cryptocurrencies allows individuals to bypass intermediaries, reducing transaction costs and empowering them to manage their wealth without dependence on third parties.

Moreover, understanding the principles of blockchain technology, the foundation of cryptocurrencies, enables individuals to appreciate the transparency and security it provides. Knowledgeable investors can make informed decisions, distinguishing between legitimate projects and potential scams, thus safeguarding their hard-earned money.

Particularly in areas that have limited access to banking services, cryptocurrencies have the potential to foster financial inclusion. Understanding how cryptocurrencies operate and how to access and use them opens up new avenues for individuals who lack access to traditional banking infrastructure. With just an internet connection, anyone can participate in the global financial ecosystem, fostering economic opportunities and breaking down barriers.

For the unbanked and underbanked populations, cryptocurrencies can serve as a lifeline, providing access to financial services, remittances, and cross-border transactions that were previously unattainable. By understanding cryptocurrencies, individuals can participate in the global economy on their terms, regardless of geographical location or socioeconomic status.

The global economy could change as a result of cryptocurrencies and blockchain technology. The ability to respond to an ever-shifting landscape and seize the opportunities it presents depends on individuals, organizations, and policymakers being aware of their consequences.

For businesses, accepting cryptocurrencies as a form of payment can open up new markets and customer bases. Companies can also leverage blockchain technology to streamline supply chains, enhance transparency, and reduce operational inefficiencies.

Additionally, understanding cryptocurrencies' role in decentralized finance (DeFi) can unlock novel financial services independent of traditional banking institutions, such as lending, borrowing, and earning interest on digital assets. DeFi has the potential to democratize financial services and provide alternatives to traditional financial intermediaries.

Cryptocurrency adoption also necessitates an awareness of personal and financial security measures. As digital assets, cryptocurrencies are susceptible to cyberattacks and scams. Understanding how to securely store cryptocurrencies in wallets, practice good password hygiene, and avoid phishing attempts is vital for safeguarding one's wealth. Moreover, awareness of potential risks and vulnerabilities in cryptocurrency can help individuals identify red flags and avoid fraudulent schemes. Educated investors are less likely to fall victim to Ponzi schemes, phishing attacks, or other malicious activities that could lead to financial losses.

Cryptocurrencies' price volatility is well-known, which can present both opportunities and risks. Understanding market dynamics and risk management strategies is essential for navigating highly unpredictable cryptocurrency markets. Knowledgeable investors can differentiate between short-term speculation and long-term investment strategies. Diversification across different cryptocurrencies and asset classes can help mitigate risks and preserve capital in the face of market downturns.

As cryptocurrencies gain mainstream acceptance, governments and regulatory bodies face the challenge of developing appropriate regulatory frameworks. It is possible for authorities to find a balance between promoting innovation and safeguarding consumers and investors by having an understanding of the complexity of cryptocurrencies. Regions can create well-informed and balanced policies by engaging with the cryptocurrency community and gaining insights into its potential benefits and risks. Responsible regulation can enhance investor confidence, encourage legitimate projects, and foster a conducive environment for the sustainable growth of the cryptocurrency ecosystem.

Understanding cryptocurrencies is not just about financial empowerment; it also involves embracing technological advancement. Blockchain technology has far-reaching applications beyond digital currencies, including supply chain management, identity verification, voting systems, etc. As individuals and businesses adopt cryptocurrencies and blockchain-based solutions, they contribute to these technologies' broader adoption and evolution. Embracing innovation encourages further research and development, propelling the world toward a more decentralized, transparent, and efficient future.

The importance of understanding cryptocurrencies cannot be overstated. It transcends the realm of personal finance and extends to the global economy, financial inclusion, and technological progress. Empowered with knowledge, individuals can seize cryptocurrency opportunities while safeguarding themselves from potential risks. Moreover, understanding cryptocurrencies is instrumental in fostering a responsible and well-regulated environment that supports innovation and inclusive growth. As the world continues to evolve in the digital age, embracing cryptocurrencies and blockchain technology is not just an option but a necessity for staying informed and actively participating in shaping the future of finance and technology.

CHAPTER II

History of Cryptocurrencies

The Origin of Cryptocurrencies

The genesis of cryptocurrencies marks a transformative moment in the history of finance and technology. Cryptocurrencies emerged as a response to traditional financial systems' shortcomings, aiming to decentralize control, enhance security, and revolutionize transactions. The history of cryptocurrencies will be examined in this section, along with the events and concepts that shaped the development of the initial decentralized digital currency and ushered in a new era of financial innovation.

To understand the origin of cryptocurrencies, we must trace their roots back to the Cypherpunk movement of the late 20th century. The Cypherpunks were a group of cryptography enthusiasts and privacy advocates who sought to promote individual freedom and privacy through the use of cryptographic tools. Their ideas and ideologies laid the groundwork for the concepts that underpin cryptocurrencies.

The Cypherpunks' vision was centered on creating cryptographic systems that would enable secure communication and financial transactions while preserving anonymity and privacy. Their pursuit of a decentralized, encrypted, and privacy-centric digital world set the stage for the emergence of cryptocurrencies.

The publication of a whitepaper in 2008 titled "Bitcoin: A Peer-to-Peer Electronic Cash System" marks a significant turning point in the development of cryptocurrencies.

Authored by an anonymous individual or group using the pseudonym Satoshi Nakamoto, the whitepaper outlined the blueprint for a decentralized peer-to-peer digital currency that would operate without central authorities.

Bitcoin's revolutionary design combined elements of the Cypherpunk movement, cryptographic principles, and innovative game theory to create an immutable and transparent ledger known as the blockchain. The whitepaper offered a consensus mechanism called proof-of-work that guaranteed the decentralized network's security and integrity through cryptographic techniques.

Satoshi Nakamoto mined the "genesis block" or "block zero," the first block of the Bitcoin blockchain, on January 3, 2009. On the block of information, it was said that "The Times 03/Jan/2009 Chancellor on brink of second bailout for banks." This timestamped headline from a British newspaper served as a symbolic nod to the motivation behind creating a decentralized alternative to the traditional financial system.

With the genesis block, Bitcoin officially became the first decentralized digital currency. The concept of a trustless, censorship-resistant, and transparent monetary system struck a chord with a growing community of developers, technologists, and individuals who saw the potential for financial liberation.

In the early days, Bitcoin attracted a small community of enthusiasts and developers who engaged in mining, trading, and promoting the new digital currency. An online community forum, Bitcointalk, became the hub for discussions and development updates.

One of the notable early Bitcoin transactions was the famous "Bitcoin Pizza Day" in May 2010. A programmer named Laszlo Hanyecz purchased two pizzas for 10,000 bitcoins, marking one of the first real-world cryptocurrency transactions.

As Bitcoin's network grew, so did its value. By 2011, it gained wider recognition, establishing the first Bitcoin exchanges and a burgeoning ecosystem of startups and businesses accepting Bitcoin as a payment method.

Following the success of Bitcoin, numerous alternative cryptocurrencies, commonly referred to as altcoins, started to emerge. These altcoins sought to address perceived limitations in Bitcoin's design or introduce novel features and use cases.

Litecoin, launched in 2011 by Charlie Lee, was one of the earliest altcoins, featuring faster block generation and a different hashing algorithm. Other altcoins like Namecoin, Ripple (later rebranded to XRP), and Peercoin brought unique features such as decentralized domain name registration, fast and low-cost cross-border transactions, and proof-of-stake consensus mechanisms.

The proliferation of altcoins demonstrated the broader potential of blockchain technology beyond a digital currency. These developments fueled a wave of innovation and experimentation within the cryptocurrency space.

In 2017, Initial Coin Offerings (ICOs) became a fundraising method for cryptocurrency projects. ICOs allowed startups to issue and distribute their own digital tokens in exchange for funding. This concept of tokenization expanded the use cases for blockchain technology beyond currency, enabling the representation of real-world assets and the creation of decentralized applications (DApps).

However, the ICO boom also led to fraudulent schemes and scams, leading to regulatory scrutiny and a shift towards more responsible token sales and fundraising models.

In recent years, the cryptocurrency space has witnessed the rapid growth of decentralized finance (DeFi). DeFi is a suite of financial services and applications built on blockchain networks, enabling lending, borrowing, and trading without intermediaries. DeFi protocols operate through smart contracts, removing the need for traditional financial institutions and centralized control.

DeFi has demonstrated the potential to disrupt traditional financial systems by providing greater accessibility, transparency, and inclusivity. However, it also presents new challenges related to security and regulation. As cryptocurrencies and blockchain technology evolve, the future remains uncertain but promising. Ongoing research and development focus on addressing scalability, energy efficiency, and user experience challenges. The transition to proof-of-stake mechanisms and layer 2 scaling solutions aims to make cryptocurrencies more sustainable and scalable.

Furthermore, central banks and governments are exploring the concept of central bank digital currencies (CBDCs) to digitize fiat currencies while retaining control and regulation. CBDCs can close the gap between traditional finance and cryptocurrencies, presenting fresh financial innovation and integration opportunities. Cryptography, decentralized networks, and a desire for a more open and transparent financial system came together to give rise to cryptocurrencies. With the release of the Bitcoin whitepaper, the world witnessed the birth of the first decentralized digital currency, setting off a chain reaction of innovation and adoption. Cryptocurrencies have grown into a diverse ecosystem with many use cases beyond digital currency, including DeFi, NFTs, and decentralized applications. While the journey has been filled with challenges and uncertainties, the potential of cryptocurrencies and blockchain technology to reshape finance, promote financial inclusion, and empower individuals must be addressed.

As the world embraces this technological revolution, it is crucial to approach cryptocurrencies with a balanced understanding of their benefits and risks. With responsible adoption, regulation, and innovation, cryptocurrencies promise to reshape the future of finance and empower individuals across the globe.

Evolution of Blockchain Technology

The evolution of blockchain technology has been nothing short of revolutionary, transforming various industries and disrupting traditional systems since its inception. Originally conceived as the underlying technology behind Bitcoin, blockchain has evolved into a powerful and versatile tool with applications beyond digital currencies. In this section, we will explore the fascinating journey of blockchain technology, from its humble beginnings as a decentralized ledger for transactions to its current status as a game-changing innovation with potential implications across multiple sectors.

The Bitcoin whitepaper, published in 2008 by a group or individual who was unidentified using the alias Satoshi Nakamoto, is where the idea for blockchain technology first emerged. The whitepaper proposed a revolutionary digital currency that operated on a decentralized peer-to-peer network, using a cryptographic technique called the blockchain to ensure the security and immutability of transactions.

At its core, the blockchain is a distributed and tamper-proof ledger that records all transactions in a chronological sequence of blocks. Each block is connected to the previous one through cryptographic hashes, creating a blockchain containing a complete transaction history. High security and transparency are provided by this structure, which makes it nearly impossible to change historical records without modifying the entire chain.

While Bitcoin was the first successful application of blockchain technology, it soon became apparent that this innovative concept had broader potential beyond digital currencies. Developers and visionaries began to explore the idea of using blockchain for various applications, aiming to create a decentralized and trustless environment for exchanging and recording data.

One of the earliest examples of blockchain expansion came with Namecoin, launched in 2011. Namecoin introduced a decentralized domain name registration system, showing that blockchain could be used for more than just financial transactions.

The next major milestone in the evolution of blockchain technology came with the introduction of Ethereum in 2015. Founded by Vitalik Buterin, Ethereum was designed to be a programmable blockchain platform, allowing developers to create and deploy smart contracts – self-executing agreements with predefined rules and conditions.

Decentralized apps (DApps) and decentralized autonomous organizations (DAOs) were made possible by smart contracts, which opened up new possibilities for blockchain technology. With Ethereum, developers could build various blockchain-based applications, from decentralized finance (DeFi) platforms to non-fungible token (NFT) marketplaces.

The need to overcome some of blockchain technology's fundamental difficulties increased along with the technology's growth. Two significant challenges that emerged were interoperability and scalability.
The capacity of several blockchains to communicate and exchange data is referred to as interoperability. Projects

like Polkadot, Cosmos, and ICON were introduced to enable seamless data transfer and value exchange between blockchains. These interoperability protocols aimed to create a network of interconnected blockchains, promoting cross-chain collaboration and data sharing.

Scalability was another crucial issue that arose as blockchain networks faced limitations in processing a high volume of transactions. Solutions like sharding, layer 2 scaling, and proof-of-stake mechanisms were proposed to improve blockchain scalability and reduce congestion.

Blockchain technology opened up a new era of tokenization – the representation of real-world assets as digital tokens on the blockchain. This breakthrough brought various assets, such as real estate, art, and commodities, onto decentralized platforms, enhancing liquidity and accessibility.

Tokenization also facilitated the creation of security tokens, offering digital representations of traditional securities like stocks and bonds. With the help of security tokens, which offer fractional ownership, investors can more easily diversify their portfolios and gain access to previously illiquid assets.

One of the most essential uses of blockchain technology that has transformed the conventional financial environment is decentralized finance (DeFi). DeFi protocols use smart contracts to offer a range of financial services without using traditional intermediaries like banks, which include lending, borrowing, decentralized exchanges, and yield farming.

The DeFi movement showcased the potential of blockchain technology to democratize finance, providing financial services to people worldwide, including those who are unbanked or underbanked. However, DeFi also introduced new security, regulation, and sustainability challenges.

Non-fungible tokens (NFTs) gained massive popularity recently, highlighting blockchain's potential to revolutionize the art and entertainment industries. NFTs are unique digital tokens representing ownership of digital assets, such as artwork, music, videos, and virtual real estate.

Through blockchain technology, NFTs provide provenance, verifiable ownership, and scarcity for digital assets, creating a new paradigm for digital ownership and monetization. The NFT boom attracted artists, creators, and collectors, sparking new possibilities for the digital economy.

As blockchain technology continued to grow, so did concerns about its environmental impact, especially in the case of proof-of-work (PoW) consensus mechanisms. PoW requires significant computational power, leading to high energy consumption and environmental strain.

In response, many blockchain projects began exploring alternative consensus mechanisms, such as proof-of-stake (PoS), which consume significantly less energy. PoS aims to improve the sustainability of blockchain networks while maintaining security and decentralization.

The acceptance of blockchain technology expanded beyond the cryptocurrency and tech communities as governments and major corporations recognized its potential. Countries began exploring using blockchain for public services, supply chain management, and voting systems.

Major companies from various industries, including finance, healthcare, and logistics, began piloting blockchain-based solutions to enhance their operations' security, transparency, and efficiency.

Despite its rapid growth and widespread adoption, blockchain technology still faces several challenges.

Regulatory uncertainty, interoperability issues, scalability, and user experience require further attention and development.

As blockchain technology evolves, researchers and developers are actively working on solving these challenges. Layer 2 scaling solutions, improved consensus mechanisms, and advancements in user-friendly interfaces hold promise for the future of blockchain technology.

The evolution of blockchain technology from the inception of Bitcoin to its current state as a transformative force across industries is a testament to human ingenuity and innovation. From enabling peer-to-peer digital currency transactions to revolutionizing finance with DeFi and tokenization, blockchain has opened up new possibilities for decentralized and transparent systems.

As blockchain technology evolves, it is crucial to address scalability, interoperability, and sustainability challenges. Responsible adoption, regulatory clarity, and ongoing research and development will be instrumental in harnessing the full potential of blockchain technology and driving it towards a more inclusive, secure, and efficient future. The journey of blockchain technology is far from over, and as it continues to evolve, it holds the potential to reshape various aspects of our lives and usher in a new era of technological advancement.

Key Milestones in Cryptocurrency Development

The development of cryptocurrencies has been marked by a series of significant milestones that have shaped the trajectory of this revolutionary financial innovation. From the release of Bitcoin's whitepaper to the rise of decentralized finance (DeFi), each milestone represents a crucial step in the evolution of cryptocurrencies and their underlying blockchain technology. In this section, we will explore some key milestones in cryptocurrency development, shedding light on the pivotal moments that have propelled this disruptive technology into the mainstream.

The first step in the history of cryptocurrencies was publishing the "Bitcoin: A Peer-to-Peer Electronic Cash System" whitepaper by an individual or group utilizing the pseudonym Satoshi Nakamoto in 2008. The whitepaper introduced the concept of a decentralized digital currency operating on a peer-to-peer network, secured by a revolutionary technology called blockchain.

Bitcoin's whitepaper laid the foundation for a decentralized, censorship-resistant, and transparent monetary system. It provided an alternative to traditional financial systems controlled by central authorities, sparking interest and curiosity among technologists, economists, and libertarians worldwide.

On January 3, 2009, Bitcoin was officially born when the first block of the blockchain, known as the "genesis block" or "block zero," was mined by Satoshi Nakamoto. On the block of information, it was said that "The Times 03/Jan/2009 Chancellor on brink of second bailout for banks" was included in the genesis block as a representation of the global financial crisis and the decentralized nature of Bitcoin as an alternative to existing banking institutions.

The mining of the genesis block marked the commencement of the Bitcoin network and its underlying blockchain, setting the stage for creating the first decentralized digital currency.

One of the most iconic milestones in cryptocurrency development was the famous "Bitcoin Pizza Day." On May 22, 2010, programmer Laszlo Hanyecz made history by using 10,000 bitcoins to purchase two pizzas. This transaction, arranged via an online forum, was the first instance of a real-world Bitcoin purchase.

The significance of Bitcoin Pizza Day lies in demonstrating the potential of cryptocurrencies as a medium of exchange. While the value of those 10,000 bitcoins has appreciated significantly since then, this milestone highlighted the practical application of digital currencies in everyday transactions.

Following the success of Bitcoin, the cryptocurrency landscape saw the emergence of alternative digital currencies, commonly known as altcoins. These altcoins introduced various improvements and innovations beyond Bitcoin's original design.

Litecoin, created by Charlie Lee and launched in 2011, was one of the earliest and most influential altcoins. Litecoin aimed to address some of the perceived limitations of Bitcoin, offering faster block generation and a different hashing algorithm.

Other notable altcoins that followed include Namecoin, which introduced a decentralized domain name system, and Ripple (later rebranded to XRP), which focused on providing fast and low-cost cross-border transactions for financial institutions.

Ethereum, introduced in 2015 by Vitalik Buterin and others, marked a significant milestone in cryptocurrency development. Unlike Bitcoin, which primarily served as a digital currency, Ethereum is a decentralized platform designed for developing and deploying decentralized applications (DApps) and smart contracts.

Smart contracts are self-executing agreements with predefined rules and conditions, operating on the Ethereum blockchain. They enable the creation of a wide range of decentralized applications, from decentralized finance (DeFi) protocols to non-fungible token (NFT) marketplaces.

The launch of Ethereum paved the way for an explosion of innovation and creativity within the cryptocurrency space, driving the development of numerous blockchain-based applications and ecosystems.

With the rise of Ethereum and the concept of smart contracts, Initial Coin Offerings (ICOs) emerged as a new method for fundraising in the cryptocurrency space. ICOs enabled blockchain projects to raise funds by issuing their digital tokens in exchange for investment.

The ICO boom of 2017 saw a proliferation of new projects, ranging from ambitious blockchain startups to speculative and fraudulent schemes. While ICOs provided an alternative fundraising mechanism, they raised concerns about regulatory compliance, investor protection, and scam risks.

One of the most transformative milestones in cryptocurrency development was the rise of decentralized finance (DeFi). DeFi refers to a suite of financial services and applications built on blockchain networks, aiming to replace traditional financial intermediaries with code-based protocols and smart contracts.

DeFi protocols offer various services, including lending, borrowing, decentralized exchanges, and yield farming. These decentralized financial applications enable users to interact with the financial system without relying on banks or other centralized entities.

By democratizing access to financial services, the DeFi movement has grown enormously, attracting billions of dollars in total value locked (TVL) and transforming the future of finance.

Non-fungible tokens (NFTs) emerged as a significant milestone in the cryptocurrency space, revolutionizing the concept of digital ownership and monetization. NFTs are unique digital tokens representing ownership of distinct digital or real-world assets, such as artwork, music, videos, and virtual real estate.

Through blockchain technology, NFTs provide provenance, verifiable ownership, and scarcity for digital assets, making it possible to authenticate and trade one-of-a-kind creations in the digital world.

With artists, creators, and collectors embracing the technology to preserve and monetize digital art and other creative works, the NFT industry has grown exponentially.

As the cryptocurrency space gained prominence, central banks worldwide began exploring the concept of central bank digital currencies (CBDCs). A CBDC represents a digital form of sovereign money issued and regulated by the central bank.

CBDCs seek to digitize traditional fiat currencies, offering potential benefits such as increased payment efficiency, financial inclusion, and greater monetary policy control. However, they also raise concerns about privacy, financial surveillance, and potential disruption to commercial banks' roles.

As cryptocurrencies gained mainstream attention, the environmental impact of energy-intensive proof-of-work (PoW) consensus mechanisms became a significant concern. PoW mining requires substantial computational power, leading to high energy consumption and carbon emissions.

In response, the cryptocurrency community has been exploring alternative consensus mechanisms, such as proof-of-stake (PoS), which consume significantly less energy while maintaining security and decentralization.

The evolution of cryptocurrencies has been characterized by a series of transformative milestones that have reshaped the global financial landscape. From the inception of Bitcoin's whitepaper to the rise of DeFi and NFTs, each milestone represents a remarkable achievement in advancing the potential of blockchain technology.

The journey of cryptocurrencies is far from over, with ongoing research and development focused on addressing scalability, interoperability, sustainability, and regulatory challenges. Responsible adoption, regulation, and innovation will be instrumental in harnessing the full potential of cryptocurrencies and blockchain technology, paving the way for a more inclusive, secure, and efficient future. The milestones achieved thus far are a testament to human ingenuity and the capacity to innovate, driving the world towards a more decentralized and digitally empowered era.

CHAPTER III

How Cryptocurrencies Work

Blockchain Fundamentals

Blockchain technology has emerged as one of the most disruptive and transformative innovations of the 21st century. Rooted in the principles of decentralization, transparency, and immutability, blockchain has the potential to revolutionize various industries and redefine the way we interact, transact, and trust in the digital age. In this section, we will delve into the fundamentals of blockchain technology, exploring its architecture, consensus mechanisms, security features, and real-world applications to understand its revolutionary impact on the modern world.

A blockchain's fundamental component is a decentralized, distributed ledger that retains a record of every transaction made among a network of computers, or nodes. Each transaction is contained in a block, and blocks are connected to one another in a chronological order to form a chain, thus the name "blockchain."

Every participant in the blockchain network maintains a copy of the entire ledger, ensuring that no single entity has control over the data. This decentralized architecture makes it resilient against single points of failure, reducing the risk of data manipulation or censorship.

Blockchain networks utilize consensus mechanisms to maintain the integrity of the blockchain and validate transactions without the need for a central authority. Consensus mechanisms enable nodes to agree on the validity of transactions and reach a common consensus on the state of the blockchain.

The most well-known consensus mechanism is proof-of-work (PoW), which Bitcoin introduced. A new block can be added to the blockchain in a PoW system by the first miner to successfully solve a challenging mathematical puzzle. The blockchain is secure but uses a lot of energy because this process calls for a lot of computational power.

Another popular consensus mechanism is proof-of-stake (PoS), where validators are chosen to create new blocks based on the number of tokens they "stake" or lock up as collateral. PoS is more energy-efficient than PoW and promotes network security through token ownership.

The immutability of blockchain technology, which guarantees that once data is stored in a block, it cannot be changed or erased, is one of its main characteristics. An unbroken chain of linked data is created because each block includes a cryptographic hash of the one before it. To

tamper with the data, an attacker must alter the block in question and all subsequent blocks, making it computationally infeasible. This immutability fosters trust in the data recorded on the blockchain, making it a reliable and secure system for storing sensitive information.

Blockchain systems are fundamentally designed with cryptography as a means of ensuring user privacy and security. By cryptographically signing transactions on the blockchain, the sender ensures that only the intended receiver can access the transaction data.

Public-key cryptography enables users to generate a pair of cryptographic keys – public and private keys. While the private key is kept private, the public key is publicly shared. A transaction is signed by the sender using their private key, and it is authenticated by the recipient using their public key.

Cryptographic hash functions are also used to generate fixed-length, unique hashes for each block and transaction. These hashes serve as digital fingerprints, enabling easy data integrity verification and preventing unauthorized changes to the blockchain.

Three basic categories can be used to classify blockchain networks: public, private, and consortium (permissioned). Each type has its unique characteristics and use cases.

Public blockchains, like Bitcoin and Ethereum, are open and permissionless, allowing anyone to participate as a node, validate transactions, and read and write data. Public blockchains prioritize decentralization and transparency, making them ideal for applications that require global accessibility and censorship resistance.

On the other hand, private blockchains are closed networks where only selected participants have access to the blockchain. Enterprises and organizations often use them to maintain privacy and restrict access to sensitive information.

A collection of pre-approved entities (consortium members) act as nodes and jointly maintain the blockchain in consortium blockchains, which are a hybrid of public and private blockchains. Consortium blockchains balance decentralization and privacy, making them suitable for applications involving multiple stakeholders but requiring a certain level of control and confidentiality.

Smart contracts are self-executing agreements with predefined rules and conditions. They operate on the blockchain and automatically execute when specific conditions are met. Ethereum popularized smart contracts and has since become a fundamental aspect of many blockchain networks.

The programmable nature of smart contracts opens up a wide range of possibilities, enabling developers to build decentralized applications (DApps) and complex financial instruments within the blockchain ecosystem.
Blockchain technology has extended its influence to various industries, driving innovation and efficiency in multiple sectors.

In finance, blockchain facilitates faster and more cost-effective cross-border payments and remittances. Decentralized finance (DeFi) platforms built on blockchain networks provide users access to lending, borrowing, and trading services without intermediaries.

In supply chain management, blockchain enhances transparency and traceability, enabling stakeholders to track the origin and movement of goods in real-time, reducing fraud and ensuring product authenticity.
The healthcare sector benefits from blockchain's secure data storage and interoperability features, improving patient data management, and ensuring the privacy of sensitive medical records.
Blockchain is also transforming the art and entertainment industries through NFTs, enabling digital artists, musicians, and content creators to tokenize and monetize their work, revolutionizing digital ownership.
Although it has great potential, blockchain technology still has a number of issues that need to be resolved before it can be widely used.

Scalability remains a significant concern, as the throughput of most blockchain networks is limited compared to traditional centralized systems. Solutions like sharding, layer 2 scaling, and improved consensus algorithms are being explored to address this challenge.

Interoperability between blockchain networks is also crucial to enable seamless data transfer and value exchange across blockchains. Interoperability protocols aim to establish a network of interconnected blockchains to facilitate cross-chain communication.

Additionally, regulatory frameworks and legal considerations must be addressed to provide a clear path for blockchain integration into existing legal systems and financial regulations.

Blockchain technology has evolved from the release of Bitcoin's whitepaper to a transformative force with far-reaching applications across industries. The fundamentals of blockchain, including its decentralized architecture, consensus mechanisms, security features, and real-world applications, have contributed to its disruptive impact on finance, supply chain management, healthcare, art, and more.

As blockchain technology advances, overcoming scalability, interoperability, and regulation challenges will be essential for mainstream adoption. Utilizing blockchain technology to its full potential and achieving its goal of a decentralized, open, and efficient global infrastructure will require responsible implementation and future innovation. With blockchain fundamentals as a strong foundation, the world is poised to embrace the decentralized revolution and embark on a new technological advancement and transformation era.

Cryptographic Principles

Cryptographic principles have been instrumental in securing sensitive information and enabling secure communication throughout history. As data becomes increasingly valuable and vulnerable in the digital age, cryptographic techniques are crucial in ensuring confidentiality, integrity, and authenticity. In this section, we will explore the basic principles of cryptography, its historical significance, modern cryptographic algorithms, and its applications in safeguarding information in the ever-evolving digital landscape.

Ancient civilizations used secret communication for military and diplomatic objectives, and this can be seen as the origin of cryptography. Early cryptographic techniques, such as Caesar cipher, substitution ciphers, and transposition ciphers, involved substituting or rearranging characters to conceal the original message. During the Renaissance, developing more sophisticated techniques, such as the Vigenère cipher, marked a significant advancement in cryptography. The Vigenère cipher introduced the concept of using a keyword for encryption, making it more challenging to break the code.

The same key is used for both encryption and decryption in symmetric cryptography, commonly referred to as secret-key cryptography. In this approach, the sender and receiver must share the secret key in advance to secure communication.

The Data Encryption Standard (DES), introduced in the 1970s, was one of the earliest symmetric encryption algorithms widely adopted for securing data. However, as computational power increased, DES was deemed vulnerable to brute-force attacks due to its small key size.

In order to solve the limitations of DES, the Advanced Encryption Standard (AES) was created in the late 1990s. AES employs symmetric key cryptography and is widely used today for its robust security and efficiency.
A revolutionary advancement in cryptography was public-key cryptography, also referred to as asymmetric

cryptography. Public-key cryptography, developed by Martin Hellman, Whitfield Diffie, and Ralph Merkle in the middle of the 1970s, enabled secure communication without the requirement of a shared secret key.

In public-key cryptography, each user possesses a pair of cryptographic keys – public and private keys. The public key is openly shared, while the private key remains confidential. Only the recipient's corresponding private key can be used to decrypt messages that have been encrypted using their public key.

The RSA algorithm, invented by Ron Rivest, Adi Shamir, and Leonard Adleman, is one of the most widely used public-key cryptographic algorithms. It is based on the large prime numbers mathematical properties and remains a cornerstone of secure communication on the internet.

Cryptographic hash functions are essential cryptographic tools that convert variable-length input into a fixed-size output, known as a hash value or digest. These hash functions are designed to be one-way and irreversible, meaning it is nearly impossible to reconstruct the original input from its hash value.

The primary application of cryptographic hash functions is to ensure data integrity. By generating a hash value for a piece of data, any modification or tampering with the data will result in a different hash value, alerting users to potential unauthorized changes.

SHA-256 (Secure Hash Algorithm 256-bit) is one of the most widely used cryptographic hash functions, playing a critical role in blockchain technology and securing digital certificates.

Digital signatures are a crucial component of public-key cryptography, providing authentication and non-repudiation for digital documents or messages. A digital signature is created by applying the sender's private key to a hash value of the document, and the recipient can verify the signature's authenticity using the sender's public key.

Digital signatures firmly guarantee that the claimed sender signed the document or message and that the content has not been altered since signing. They are widely used in electronic transactions, authentication protocols, and secure communications.

Robust key management is essential to cryptographic systems' security. Asymmetric cryptography relies on the secure distribution and protection of private keys, while symmetric cryptography requires secure key exchange between parties.

Certificate authorities (CAs) is significant in key management for public-key cryptography. CAs issue digital certificates, which include the public key and other identifying information about the certificate holder. These certificates are used to verify the authenticity of public keys and facilitate secure communication between parties.

In the digital age, the widespread use of the internet and connected devices has introduced new challenges for cryptographic principles. The rapid growth of data, the increasing sophistication of cyberattacks, and the emergence of quantum computing pose threats to traditional cryptographic algorithms.

Researchers are creating quantum-resistant algorithms for cryptography that can withstand attacks from quantum computers to overcome these issues. Post-quantum cryptography aims to ensure the continued security of digital communication, even in the presence of powerful quantum computers.

Homomorphic encryption, a cutting-edge cryptographic technique, also allows computations on encrypted data without decryption, providing a revolutionary approach to secure data processing.

Cryptographic principles find applications in various domains, safeguarding sensitive information and enabling secure communication.

In secure communication, cryptographic protocols like Secure Sockets Layer (SSL) and Transport Layer Security (TLS) protect data transmitted over the internet, ensuring privacy and authenticity of websites.

In digital currencies and blockchain technology, cryptographic principles are fundamental to securing transactions, digital signatures, and ensuring the integrity of the blockchain ledger.

Cryptographic principles also play a vital role in secure email communication, digital rights management (DRM), secure online voting systems, and securing data at rest and in transit.

While cryptographic principles have enabled secure communication and data protection, they also raise ethical considerations. On one hand, cryptography empowers individuals to safeguard their privacy and protect sensitive information. On the other hand, it can also be misused for illicit activities, such as concealing criminal behavior or terrorist activities.

Balancing the need for security and privacy with law enforcement and public safety concerns poses a challenge for policymakers and society. Striking the right balance requires responsible use of cryptography, adherence to legal frameworks, and continuous efforts to stay ahead of evolving threats.

Cryptographic principles have been instrumental in safeguarding information and securing communication throughout history, evolving from ancient ciphers to modern cryptographic algorithms. Symmetric and public-key cryptography, cryptographic hash functions, and digital signatures are the building blocks underpinning data security in the digital age.

As the digital landscape evolves, cryptographic principles will play an increasingly crucial role in protecting sensitive information and ensuring trust and security in the digital realm. Responsible use of cryptography and continued research and development of new cryptographic solutions will be essential to maintain data confidentiality, integrity, and authenticity in the ever-changing digital landscape. By embracing and understanding cryptographic principles, society can unlock the full potential of secure and private communication while addressing the challenges of the digital era with integrity and responsibility.

Mining and Consensus Mechanisms

Mining and consensus mechanisms are foundational components of blockchain technology, serving as the backbone of decentralized networks. These mechanisms play a critical role in achieving agreement among network participants and securing the integrity of blockchain transactions. In this section, we will explore the concepts of mining and consensus mechanisms, their historical context, different types of consensus algorithms, and their role in ensuring trust and security in decentralized systems.

Mining is fundamental in many blockchain networks, particularly those that use proof-of-work (PoW) consensus mechanisms. Using computational power, mining includes validating blockchain transactions and solving challenging mathematical puzzles.

The right to add a new block of transactions to a proof-of-work (PoW) blockchain belongs to the first miner to figure out the puzzle. This process is resource-intensive and requires significant computational power, making it economically costly and time-consuming.

Bitcoin's creator, Satoshi Nakamoto, introduced the concept of mining as a means of reaching consensus in a decentralized network without relying on a central authority. Through mining, miners contribute their computational resources to maintain the blockchain's integrity and security.

While various blockchains have widely adopted PoW, it has limitations, including high energy consumption and potential centralization risks. As a result, alternative consensus mechanisms, such as proof-of-stake (PoS), have gained traction in the blockchain community.

In PoS, validators, also known as stakeholders, are chosen to create new blocks based on the number of tokens they "stake" or lock up as collateral. Validators are selected to develop blocks deterministically, considering the amount of tokens staked and the length of time they have been held.

Compared to PoW, PoS is thought to be more ecologically friendly and energy-efficient. By selecting validators based on their network stake rather than their computational power, it also lowers the risk of centralization.

Delegated proof-of-stake (DPoS) is a variation of PoS that introduces a governance layer to the consensus process. Stakeholders in DPoS-based blockchains vote to choose a small number of delegates who are in charge of validating transactions and generating new blocks.

DPoS aims to improve network efficiency and scalability by delegating block validation to a smaller number of trusted delegates. Delegates are expected to act in the network's best interest and may be subject to recall if they do not fulfill their responsibilities adequately.

Projects like EOS and Tron have adopted DPoS to achieve faster transaction processing times and higher throughput, making them suitable for applications requiring many transactions per second.

Practical Byzantine Fault Tolerance, or PBFT is a consensus algorithm that targets high-performance and low-latency blockchain networks. PBFT is primarily used in permissioned blockchains, where a limited number of known participants can participate in the consensus process.

In PBFT, a leader is chosen to propose a new block, and other nodes in the network validate the proposed block. A two-phase process is followed to achieve consensus: a prepare phase and a commit phase. It is considered committed if two-thirds of the nodes agree on the proposed block.

PBFT provides fast transaction finality and is highly fault-tolerant, allowing the blockchain to continue functioning correctly even if some nodes are compromised or fail to respond.

Mining and consensus mechanisms have practical applications in various domains, enabling secure and decentralized solutions.

In cryptocurrencies, mining is crucial in validating transactions and adding new blocks to the blockchain. In exchange for their efforts in safeguarding the network, miners are rewarded with freshly created coins and transaction fees.

Consensus mechanisms find applications beyond cryptocurrencies. In supply chain management, blockchain networks with PoW or PoS consensus can ensure transparency and traceability, enabling stakeholders to track the origin and movement of goods.

In decentralized finance (DeFi), PoS-based blockchains power lending and borrowing platforms, decentralized exchanges, and yield farming protocols, offering users financial services without relying on traditional intermediaries.

The development of blockchain technology has witnessed the evolution of various consensus mechanisms, each designed to address specific challenges and requirements.

Efforts have been made to improve the scalability and energy efficiency of PoW through concepts like mining algorithms with lower energy consumption, such as proof-of-space (PoSpace) and proof-of-capacity (PoC). Additionally, consensus mechanisms that combine elements of PoW and PoS, such as delegated proof-of-authority (DPoA) and hybrid consensus, aim to strike a balance between security and scalability.

Despite the progress made in consensus mechanisms, challenges still need to be addressed in achieving consensus at scale and ensuring robust security.

Scalability continues to be a significant challenge for PoW-based blockchains, leading to issues with transaction throughput and higher fees during times of network congestion. Solutions like layer 2 scaling and sharding aim to improve scalability by processing transactions off-chain or dividing the blockchain into smaller partitions.

In PoS-based blockchains, challenges related to the "nothing at stake" problem and "long-range attacks" have been raised. These issues pertain to the incentives for validators to participate in consensus honestly and the potential of attackers to rewrite the blockchain history.

As blockchain technology evolves, researchers and developers are actively exploring new consensus mechanisms, such as proof-of-burn (PoB), proof-of-reputation (PoR), and proof-of-space-time (PoST), to address scalability, security, and energy efficiency challenges.

Mining, particularly in PoW-based blockchains, has drawn attention to its environmental impact due to the high energy consumption required for computational work.

Some blockchain projects have sought to address this concern by exploring alternative consensus mechanisms, such as PoS and DPoS, which are more energy-efficient and environmentally friendly.

Additionally, initiatives like renewable energy-powered mining farms and carbon-neutral mining practices have been proposed to mitigate the environmental impact of blockchain mining.

Mining and consensus mechanisms are essential pillars of blockchain technology, enabling secure and decentralized networks. From the proof-of-work mechanism introduced by Bitcoin to the evolution of proof-of-stake and delegated proof-of-stake, consensus mechanisms have evolved to meet the diverse needs of different blockchain networks.

As the blockchain landscape grows, scalability, security, and environmental challenges require innovative solutions and ongoing research. The future of mining and consensus mechanisms lies in striking a balance between efficiency, safety, and sustainability, enabling blockchain technology to mature and reach its full potential as a transformative force in the digital world. With continued development and responsible use, mining and consensus mechanisms will forge trust in decentralized networks, shaping a new era of secure and transparent transactions.

CHAPTER IV

Popular Cryptocurrencies

Bitcoin

The creation of Bitcoin in 2008 under the pseudonym Satoshi Nakamoto marked the beginning of a new era in finance. Bitcoin, the initial decentralized digital currency in the world, completely changed how we think about and use money. We will examine Bitcoin's development, history, technology, mining method, security measures, and economic impact in this section, emphasizing on how it has come to represent financial innovation and individual empowerment.

The first step in the history of Bitcoin was the publication of the "Bitcoin: A Peer-to-Peer Electronic Cash System" whitepaper in October 2008. The whitepaper established the idea of a digital currency that operates on a network that is decentralized and is supported by innovative blockchain technology.

To provide individuals full authority over their money and financial activities, Satoshi Nakamoto imagined a financial system that could do away with conventional intermediaries. Technologists, libertarians, and people seeking financial independence were all drawn to the idea of a trustless, peer-to-peer network where users could deal without intermediaries.

Blockchain, Bitcoin's underlying technology, is the key to its success. A distributed ledger known as blockchain, records every transaction securely and impenetrably. Each transaction is contained in its own block, which is then connected to other blocks chronologically to create an immutable chain of transactions.

The blockchain for Bitcoin is monitored and protected by a decentralized network of nodes (miners) worldwide. These miners validate transactions and add new blocks to the blockchain by using computational power to solve challenging mathematical puzzles.

Bitcoin utilizes a consensus mechanism called proof-of-work (PoW), in which miners compete to solve a mathematical puzzle; the first to do so earns the right to add the next block. By requiring re-mining all succeeding blocks to change a single block, this procedure protects the blockchain's security and integrity, making it nearly impossible to tamper with previous transactions.

Mining is an essential function in the Bitcoin network to keep the blockchain's integrity and create new bitcoins for circulation. To compete in the PoW process, miners employ specialized equipment and software and invest a lot of computational power to solve the puzzle.

The successful miner who successfully adds a new block to the blockchain is entitled to a set amount of bitcoins as payment for their efforts, also known as the block reward. The block reward is reduced by half every four years, or "halving," from its initial value of 50 bitcoins.

By capping the quantity at 21 million coins, the halving assures a controlled and predictable creation of new bitcoins. This element of scarcity adds to Bitcoin's appeal as a store of value, which is frequently compared to digital gold.

The distinctive qualities of Bitcoin have established it as a store of value and a digital substitute for conventional fiat currencies. Investors and individuals looking to protect themselves against inflation and financial instability have been drawn by its limited supply, decentralized nature, and resistance to censorship.

As Bitcoin's usage has increased, so has its use as a medium of exchange for products and services. Bitcoin is a widely accepted payment option by retailers worldwide, and Bitcoin ATMs make it simple to exchange Bitcoin for fiat money.

Bitcoin transactions are secure due to cryptography concepts. A public key that is disclosed publicly and a private key that is kept confidential are the two cryptographic keys that belong to each user. The sender's private key is used to cryptographically sign transactions to ensure their legitimacy, while the recipient utilizes the sender's public key to decrypt and validate the transaction.

Additionally, using cryptographic hash algorithms, Bitcoin generates distinct digital fingerprints for transactions and blocks. This feature ensures that any data modification generates an entirely new hash value, protecting the blockchain's integrity.

The fast expansion and rise in popularity of Bitcoin have created issues with scalability and transaction throughput. The Bitcoin blockchain's original design has a limited capacity to handle a huge volume of transactions, which causes network congestion and higher transaction fees during peak times.

To address these problems, the Bitcoin community has looked into ideas like the Lightning Network, a layer 2 protocol that enables quicker and more affordable microtransactions by settling them off-chain.

Additionally, debates on block size expansions, including the contentious "block size debate," have emphasized balancing decentralization and network capacity.

Bitcoin received regulatory interest as it gained popularity. Governments and financial organizations worldwide have used different strategies to control Bitcoin and other cryptocurrencies.

Some nations have welcomed Bitcoin and accepted it as a legitimate means of exchange or investment. Due to financial crime, money laundering, and consumer protection concerns, numerous states have put limitations or outright bans on its use.

With efforts to achieve a balance between supporting innovation and guaranteeing compliance with current financial regulations, the regulatory landscape for Bitcoin is constantly changing.
The global financial system has seen substantial disruptions due to Bitcoin's existence. Traditional financial intermediaries like banks and remittance businesses are put to the test by its capacity to handle cross-border transactions with lower fees and faster processing times.

Self-custody, or the idea that people control their own private keys and funds, has sparked discussions about the function of custodial services and the idea that "not your keys, not your coins."
Bitcoin has emerged as a lifeline for financial inclusion and access to international markets in areas with unstable currencies or restricted access to traditional banking.

Despite its revolutionary potential, Bitcoin has come under fire on several events. Due to its price volatility, some have questioned whether it is appropriate to use it as a reliable means of exchange.
Concerns have been expressed about the sustainability and contribution of Bitcoin mining to carbon emissions due to its negative environmental impact, mainly caused by PoW's energy consumption.

To reduce these concerns, efforts have been made to explore more energy-efficient alternatives to PoS as a consensus mechanism.

Beyond its function as a digital currency, Bitcoin has sparked a broader discussion about the direction of money and finance. Thousands of additional cryptocurrencies and blockchain-based projects have been created due to its popularity, collectively known as the "cryptocurrency and blockchain ecosystem."
Bitcoin introduced the ideas of decentralization, self-sovereignty, and financial empowerment. These ideas have since spread throughout many industries and are impacting the future of finance, government, and digital identity.

As the first cryptocurrency, Bitcoin has changed the financial landscape and sparked a worldwide discussion about the future of money. Due to its decentralized character, which was made possible by the innovative blockchain technology, the conventional banking system is now under threat.
The success of Bitcoin has been mainly due to mining and the PoW consensus mechanism, which guarantees the accuracy and security of all network transactions. The continued research and development within the Bitcoin community is paving the path for a more sustainable and effective blockchain ecosystem, even though issues with scalability and environmental concerns still exist.

Bitcoin's influence on the world economy and financial system will only grow as it develops. Discussions about decentralization, privacy, and financial inclusion in the digital age will be encouraged as it continues to catalyze financial innovation. Bitcoin has irrevocably changed the course of history as the foundation for a new financial paradigm, inspiring subsequent generations to reconsider concepts like trust, sovereignty, and money.

Ethereum

The 2015 introduction of Ethereum by Vitalik Buterin and a group of developers marked a revolutionary advancement in blockchain technology. As the world's leading decentralized platform for smart contracts and decentralized applications (DApps), Ethereum has redefined the possibilities of blockchain beyond simple financial transactions. In this section, we will explore the history, technology, smart contracts, consensus mechanism, use cases, challenges, and future prospects of Ethereum, shedding light on its pivotal role in the blockchain revolution.

The idea of Ethereum emerged in late 2013 when Vitalik Buterin, a young programmer and blockchain enthusiast, proposed the concept of a blockchain platform that could support more than just financial transactions. In late 2014, a crowdfunding campaign was launched to fund the development of Ethereum, attracting a significant response from the blockchain community.

Ethereum's development took inspiration from Bitcoin's blockchain but extended its capabilities to allow developers to create smart contracts and DApps. The official Ethereum blockchain was launched in July 2015, and since then, it has grown to become the most prominent platform for decentralized applications.

At the core of Ethereum's revolutionary capabilities lie smart contracts. Self-executing contracts with pre-established terms and conditions are known as smart contracts. They operate on the blockchain and automatically execute when specific conditions are met. Because smart contracts are programmable, developers may design decentralized systems that can handle complex interactions and procedures automatically, eliminating the need for middlemen.

The environment around Ethereum has grown to be a hub for creativity, allowing developers to create a vast array of DApps. These applications span various industries, including finance, supply chain management, gaming, identity management, and decentralized finance (DeFi). The open and permissionless nature of the Ethereum network has facilitated the rapid growth of a vibrant ecosystem of developers, entrepreneurs, and users.

The Ethereum Virtual Machine (EVM) is a critical component that enables the execution of smart contracts on the Ethereum network. It is a runtime environment that executes code written in Ethereum's native programming language, Solidity. The EVM is entirely isolated from the host operating system, ensuring security and preventing malicious code from affecting the network.

The Ethereum blockchain's smart contract deployment and execution are made simple by the EVM's architecture. It facilitates the creation of a vast array of applications, from simple token contracts to complex decentralized autonomous organizations (DAOs).

In its early days, Ethereum, like Bitcoin, used a proof-of-work (PoW) consensus mechanism to achieve agreement among network participants and secure the blockchain. Miners competed to solve complex mathematical puzzles, with the winner adding new blocks to the blockchain and receiving rewards.

However, PoW's energy-intensive nature and scalability limitations prompted the Ethereum community to explore alternatives. Ethereum is in the process of transitioning to Ethereum 2.0, a major upgrade that introduces a proof-of-stake (PoS) consensus mechanism.

In PoS, validators are chosen to create new blocks based on the number of ethers (ETH) they "stake" or lock up as collateral. Validators are rewarded for their honest participation in block validation, and their stakes serve as a guarantee against malicious behavior. Compared to PoW, PoS uses less energy and tries to make the Ethereum network more scalable.

The area of decentralized finance (DeFi) has seen the greatest influence from Ethereum. The word "DeFi" describes the network of financial apps and protocols constructed on blockchain networks that allow financial services to be provided without the need for middlemen.

Ethereum's smart contract capabilities have been instrumental in powering DeFi protocols, such as decentralized exchanges (DEXs), lending platforms, stablecoins, yield farming, and asset management tools. These applications enable users to lend, borrow, trade, and earn interest on their digital assets directly on the Ethereum blockchain.

With billions of dollars in total value locked (TVL) attracted, DeFi has experienced exponential development and grown to become a major disruptor in the conventional banking industry.

Ethereum's popularity and the surge of DeFi applications have led to challenges related to network congestion and high transaction fees. As the number of users and transactions on the network increases, Ethereum's limited capacity to process transactions has led to slower confirmation times and higher gas fees.

The issue of scalability has prompted the Ethereum community to explore various solutions. Ethereum 2.0, with its shift to PoS and the introduction of shard chains, aims to significantly improve scalability and transaction throughput.

Promising options that allow more transactions to be performed off-chain and settled on the Ethereum mainnet are Layer 2 solutions like ZK-Rollups and Optimistic Rollups.

Beyond DeFi, Ethereum has found applications in various industries, showcasing its versatility and potential to disrupt traditional systems.

Ethereum-based DApps in supply chain management facilitate transparency and traceability, enabling stakeholders to monitor the origin and flow of goods along the supply chain.

The notion of non-fungible tokens (NFTs) has been brought to the gaming industry by blockchain-based games on Ethereum, which have facilitated actual ownership of in-game assets and ushered in a new era of digital ownership.

Ethereum's decentralized identity solutions have the potential to revolutionize identity management and authentication, providing individuals with control over their personal data.

Ethereum's security is of utmost importance due to the value and sensitivity of the assets and data on the network. The Ethereum community actively contributes to the network's security by submitting and implementing Ethereum Improvement Proposals (EIPs).

EIPs are community-driven proposals to improve the Ethereum network. They cover various aspects, including security upgrades, new features, and optimizations. EIP-1559, for example, is a recent proposal aimed at changing the transaction fee structure on Ethereum to provide a more predictable fee mechanism, reduce network congestion, and potentially make the network more deflationary.

Ethereum's impact extends beyond the realm of finance and technology. Its potential as a foundational layer for the decentralized internet, often referred to as Web3, holds promise for a more open, censorship-resistant, and user-centric internet.

The concept of decentralized autonomous organizations (DAOs) built on Ethereum has sparked discussions about new models of governance and decision-making, where communities collectively manage and govern projects and resources.

As Ethereum continues to evolve, the concept of Web3 and decentralized applications may redefine how individuals interact with online services, data, and digital assets, providing a glimpse of a future internet where users fully control their digital lives.

Ethereum stands as a transformative force in the blockchain revolution, redefining the possibilities of smart contracts and decentralized applications. Its vibrant ecosystem of developers, users, and innovators has ushered in a new era of financial inclusion, digital ownership, and trustless interactions.

With the ongoing transition to Ethereum 2.0 and the exploration of Layer 2 solutions, Ethereum is addressing scalability challenges to pave the way for more efficient and sustainable blockchain applications.

As Ethereum's impact continues to expand across industries and applications, its role as a catalyst for Web3 and the decentralized internet holds the promise of a more equitable, transparent, and user-centric digital world.

As the journey of Ethereum unfolds, its potential to reshape finance, governance, and the internet at large underscores its position as a trailblazer in the ongoing transformation of our global digital landscape.

Ripple (XRP)

The innovative cryptocurrency and blockchain platform Ripple (XRP) has become a top choice for international payments and remittances. Ripple, which was established by Chris Larsen and Jed McCaleb in 2012, has become one of the most well-known blockchain networks, providing quick and affordable international transactions. This section will explore the history, technology, consensus mechanism, use cases, challenges, and potential future of Ripple (XRP), shedding light on its significant impact on the global financial landscape.

Ripple's roots can be traced back to the early days of blockchain technology when its founders sought to address the inefficiencies and high costs associated with cross-border payments. The initial idea was to develop a consensus algorithm and decentralized digital currency that would enable quicker, less expensive, and safer international transactions.

The company behind Ripple, now known as Ripple Labs, officially launched the Ripple payment protocol and its native digital asset, XRP, in 2012. Over time, Ripple's focus shifted towards providing solutions for financial institutions and banks, positioning itself as a transformative force in the realm of cross-border payments.

Unlike traditional proof-of-work (PoW) and proof-of-stake (PoS) consensus mechanisms used by many cryptocurrencies, Ripple employs a unique consensus algorithm called the Ripple Consensus Algorithm (RCA) or the XRP Ledger Consensus Protocol.

The RCA is based on the concept of distributed agreement, where a set of trusted validators determines the validity of transactions and the order in which they are included in the XRP Ledger. Validators are known and identified entities, chosen for their reliability and adherence to network rules.

The XRP Ledger is designed to achieve consensus approximately every three to five seconds, enabling fast transaction confirmation and scalability. This makes Ripple an ideal solution for real-time, cross-border transactions, where speed and certainty are crucial.

XRP, as the native digital asset of the Ripple network, plays a crucial role in facilitating cross-border transactions. It serves as a bridge currency, allowing direct exchanges between different fiat currencies without the need for traditional intermediaries like correspondent banks.

Banks must hold balances in various currencies across multiple accounts in traditional international payments to facilitate cross-border transactions. This ties up capital and increases liquidity costs. With XRP, banks and financial institutions can use it as an intermediary currency to settle transactions quickly and efficiently, reducing liquidity costs and unlocking capital.

Ripple's technology has revolutionized cross-border payments, offering significant advantages over traditional payment systems like SWIFT. The traditional system can take days to settle international transactions, involving multiple intermediaries, high fees, and potential delays.

The near-instant settlement and real-time transfers made possible by Ripple's network enhance the effectiveness and transparency of cross-border transactions. This has made Ripple an alluring option for banks and other financial organizations looking to improve their cross-border payment services and save operating expenses.

Ripple's efforts to transform cross-border payments have led to significant partnerships with leading financial institutions and banks worldwide. These partnerships have fueled the adoption of Ripple's technology, with many institutions integrating Ripple's solutions into their payment systems.

Notable partners include Santander, American Express, Standard Chartered, SBI Holdings, and PNC Bank. These partnerships have contributed to the global adoption of Ripple's technology and the recognition of XRP as a viable digital asset for international transactions.

Beyond its impact on the traditional banking sector, Ripple has also demonstrated potential in promoting financial inclusion and remittance services. A vital source of income for numerous families in developing nations is remittances, or the money sent home by people who work abroad.

Families may get far less valuable remittances due to the high costs and protracted processing times of traditional transfer systems. With its speed and cost-effectiveness, Ripple's technology has the potential to increase the value of remittances and improve financial inclusion for individuals in underserved regions.

XRP has garnered a passionate and active community of supporters, developers, and enthusiasts. The XRP community has been instrumental in promoting the use of XRP as a bridge currency for international payments and in implementing Ripple's technology.

The utility of XRP extends beyond its role in facilitating cross-border transactions. XRP can be used for micropayments, tokenizing real-world assets, and to incentivize liquidity on Ripple's network.

Despite its successes, Ripple has faced its share of challenges. The classification of XRP as a digital asset and whether it should be considered a security under certain regulatory frameworks has been a subject of debate and legal scrutiny.

Ripple has been involved in legal disputes, including a lawsuit brought by the U.S. Securities and Exchange Commission (SEC) alleging that the sale of XRP constituted an unregistered securities offering. The outcome of these legal battles may have implications for the classification and regulation of digital assets in the broader cryptocurrency industry.

As Ripple's technology gains adoption, the network's scalability and interoperability become crucial considerations. As transaction volumes increase, Ripple's network must continue to handle higher throughput while maintaining fast and secure transactions.

Interoperability with other blockchains and payment systems is also essential for Ripple's continued growth and integration into the global financial infrastructure.

As Ripple continues to navigate regulatory challenges and scale its network, the future holds great promise for the global adoption of its technology. The use of blockchain and digital assets for cross-border payments is expected to become more prevalent as financial institutions seek cost-efficient and secure solutions.
Ripple's potential impact on financial inclusion, remittance services, and emerging economies underscores its role as a transformative force in the global financial landscape.

With its fast and cost-effective blockchain technology, Ripple (XRP) has emerged as a leading solution for transforming cross-border payments and remittances. By providing a bridge currency and facilitating near-instant settlement, Ripple has revolutionized the traditional financial system, offering a glimpse of a future where cross-border transactions are seamless, transparent, and affordable.
As Ripple continues to navigate regulatory challenges and enhance its network's scalability and interoperability, its

role in promoting financial inclusion, remittance services, and global adoption of blockchain technology will be increasingly significant.

As financial institutions and businesses recognize the value of Ripple's technology, the ripple effect of its innovations will undoubtedly continue to reshape the future of cross-border payments and the global financial landscape.

Litecoin

As the "silver to Bitcoin's gold," Litecoin is a very influential cryptocurrency that was among the earliest in the digital asset ecosystem. Created by Charlie Lee in 2011, Litecoin was designed to complement Bitcoin by offering faster transaction times, lower fees, and increased scalability. In this section, we will explore the history, technology, mining process, use cases, challenges, and future prospects of Litecoin, shedding light on its significant role in the cryptocurrency space.

Litecoin's journey began in October 2011 when Charlie Lee, a former Google engineer, released the open-source code for Litecoin. Lee aimed to create a more efficient and lightweight alternative to Bitcoin, addressing some of the limitations faced by the pioneering cryptocurrency.

Inspired by Bitcoin's codebase, Litecoin shares many similarities with its predecessor, but also introduces some key differences. The Litecoin community's strong participation and early adoption have contributed to its longevity and ongoing importance in the quickly changing cryptocurrency landscape.

Litecoin's underlying technology is based on a different consensus mechanism compared to Bitcoin. Instead of using the SHA-256 algorithm for mining, Litecoin uses Scrypt, a memory-hard cryptographic algorithm. Scrypt is more resistant to specialized mining hardware referred to as ASICs (Application-Specific Integrated Circuits) since it requires more memory to compute.

The Scrypt algorithm allows Litecoin to be mined using consumer-grade hardware, making mining more accessible and decentralized compared to Bitcoin. This decision aligns with Litecoin's mission to create a more inclusive and decentralized digital currency.

Another fundamental difference is the block generation time. While Bitcoin's block time is approximately 10 minutes, Litecoin's block time is only 2.5 minutes. This faster block generation enables quicker transaction confirmation and higher transaction throughput.

Litecoin's mining process involves solving complex mathematical puzzles using computational power. The Scrypt puzzle is solved by miners competing with one another, and the first miner to do so gets to add a new block to the Litecoin blockchain.

Due to the Scrypt algorithm's memory-intensive nature, Litecoin mining is more accessible to individual miners and less dominated by large mining pools and specialized hardware. This approach aligns with Litecoin's goal of maintaining a decentralized network and reducing the risk of centralization.

Litecoin's speed and lower transaction fees have positioned it as an attractive digital payment solution. Its faster block generation time allows for quicker transaction confirmations, making it well-suited for day-to-day transactions and microtransactions.

Merchants and businesses have increasingly started accepting Litecoin as a form of payment, enhancing its utility as a digital currency. Users can send and receive Litecoin globally with minimal transaction fees, making it a viable alternative to traditional payment systems for cross-border transactions.

Litecoin implemented the Segregated Witness (SegWit) upgrade to further enhance its capabilities in 2017. SegWit is a protocol upgrade that improves transaction efficiency by separating signature data from transaction data. This reduces the size of transactions and increases the capacity of the Litecoin blockchain.

Additionally, Litecoin has embraced the Lightning Network, a second-layer protocol that enables off-chain transactions. The Lightning Network allows users to conduct fast and low-cost transactions without congesting the main blockchain. This technology enhances Litecoin's scalability and makes it even more efficient for microtransactions and small value transfers.

Litecoin's close relationship with Bitcoin is evident in several aspects. Most of Litecoin's codebase is derived from Bitcoin, making them technologically similar. Litecoin also shares a fixed supply cap with Bitcoin, with a total of 84 million Litecoins that will ever be mined.

The relationship between Litecoin and Bitcoin is often described as complementary, with Litecoin acting as a testing ground for Bitcoin's new features and upgrades. Many innovations introduced in Litecoin, such as SegWit and the Lightning Network, were later adopted by Bitcoin.

Various digital assets are competing with Litecoin as the cryptocurrency market has grown. While its early mover advantage and community support have helped it maintain its position as one of the top cryptocurrencies, it faces competition from newer projects with unique features and use cases.

Additionally, the rise of Ethereum and its smart contract capabilities has opened up new possibilities for decentralized applications beyond simple payments, potentially diverting attention and development resources away from Litecoin.

Scalability remains a crucial challenge for Litecoin, as well as for the entire cryptocurrency ecosystem. As the number of users and transactions increases, finding scalable solutions while maintaining decentralization becomes paramount.

Litecoin's future prospects also depend on its ability to attract wider adoption and use cases beyond its current niche. Collaboration with businesses, financial institutions, and developers will be essential in expanding its utility and achieving mass adoption as a digital payment solution.
Litecoin's active and passionate community has been instrumental in its continued development and growth. The community-driven approach has fostered innovation, improvements, and the integration of new features into the Litecoin network.

An important factor in fostering the growth of the Litecoin ecosystem and encouraging its global adoption is the non-profit Litecoin Foundation.

Litecoin's journey as the "silver to Bitcoin's gold" has been marked by innovation, community support, and a commitment to providing a more efficient and accessible digital payment solution. Its faster transaction times, lower fees, and Scrypt-based mining have distinguished it from its peers and solidified its place in cryptocurrency. Litecoin's focus on scalability, mass adoption, and further technological improvements will determine its long-term relevance and impact as the cryptocurrency market evolves. Litecoin remains a pioneer in the cryptocurrency space, contributing to the ongoing transformation of the global financial ecosystem.

Other Notable Cryptocurrencies

While Bitcoin and Ethereum dominate the cryptocurrency market, a diverse and ever-expanding ecosystem of other notable cryptocurrencies have made significant contributions to the blockchain revolution. From privacy-focused coins to decentralized finance (DeFi) platforms and smart contract solutions, these digital assets offer unique features and use cases that cater to specific niches and industries. In this section, we will explore some of the other notable cryptocurrencies, delving into their histories, technologies, use cases, and potential impact on the future of finance and beyond.

Developed in the year 2014 as a Bytecoin fork, Monero is distinguished by its focus on anonymity and privacy. Built on the CryptoNote protocol, Monero employs ring signatures and stealth addresses to obfuscate transaction details and protect users' identities. This privacy-focused approach has made Monero the preferred choice for users seeking to conduct confidential transactions without the risk of traceability.

Monero's fungibility, where all coins are considered interchangeable, sets it apart from Bitcoin, whose public ledger allows for transaction tracing and tainted coins. The increased demand for privacy in the digital asset space has driven Monero's popularity and its recognition as a leading privacy-centric cryptocurrency.

In order to provide a secure and scalable foundation for developing smart contracts and decentralized apps (DApps), Charles Hoskinson introduced Cardano, a decentralized platform, in 2017. The platform uses a layered architecture that separates the settlement and computation layers, allowing for increased flexibility and security.

Cardano's development is research-driven, relying on a peer-reviewed approach to ensure that innovations are rigorously tested and validated before implementation. This commitment to scientific rigor has earned Cardano a reputation for being a well-designed and technically sound blockchain platform.

With an emphasis on interoperability, scalability, and sustainability, Cardano seeks to develop into a strong ecosystem that supports companies, governments, and developers working to create decentralized solutions. Polkadot, founded by Gavin Wood, a co-founder of Ethereum, is a groundbreaking project designed to address one of the critical challenges in the blockchain space: interoperability. Launched in 2020, Polkadot aims to facilitate seamless communication and data sharing between different blockchains, allowing them to work together as a unified network.

Polkadot's unique approach relies on its relay chain, which serves as the central hub connecting multiple parachains (parallel blockchains) and allowing them to interact with each other. This interoperability feature has attracted developers and projects looking to create decentralized applications that can leverage the combined capabilities of various blockchains.

One of the biggest cryptocurrency exchanges in the world, Binance, launched Binance Coin (BNB) in 2017 as its native coin. BNB was initially presented as an ERC-20 token on the Ethereum network. Later, it moved to the Binance Chain, a blockchain that Binance constructed, utilizing the Binance Smart Chain for smart contract functionality.

The main application for BNB is as a utility token in the Binance ecosystem, where it offers advantages including reduced trading fees and access to token sales on Binance Launchpad. In addition, BNB acts as a bridge currency for cross-chain transactions and is essential to the Binance Decentralized Exchange (DEX).

The success of BNB has led to its widespread adoption beyond the Binance ecosystem, making it one of the most valuable and widely used cryptocurrencies in the market.

A distributed oracle network that links smart contracts to external APIs and real-world data is known as Chainlink. It was founded by Sergey Nazarov and Steve Ellis in 2017. Smart contracts are self-executing agreements that operate on blockchain networks but lack the ability to access data outside their respective chains.
As a bridge, Chainlink's oracle network gives smart contracts access to off-chain data, including stock prices, weather reports, and sports scores. This feature enables the execution of complex and automated agreements based on real-time and accurate data.

As smart contracts become increasingly prevalent, Chainlink's role in providing reliable and secure data inputs is becoming integral to the growth of the decentralized economy.
Uniswap, launched in 2018 by Hayden Adams, is a decentralized exchange (DEX) built on the Ethereum blockchain. Unlike traditional centralized exchanges that require custody of user funds, Uniswap operates through automated smart contracts, providing a trustless and non-custodial platform for token swaps.
Uniswap's automated market maker (AMM) model relies on liquidity pools, where users contribute their tokens to facilitate trading. In return, liquidity providers earn fees generated by the trades in the pool. This innovative approach has transformed the decentralized exchange landscape, making it accessible to anyone with an Ethereum wallet.

Uniswap's native governance token, UNI, allows users to participate in the platform's decision-making process and earn rewards for their involvement.

The high-performance blockchain platform Solana was introduced in 2020 with the goal of offering scalable and quick infrastructure for decentralized apps. Solana is built on a unique proof-of-history (PoH) consensus mechanism and achieves high throughput and low-latency transaction processing.

Solana's ability to process thousands of transactions per second has positioned it as a strong competitor in DeFi and attracted developers seeking to build complex and scalable applications.

Stellar, founded in 2014 by Jed McCaleb, is a decentralized platform designed to facilitate cross-border payments and promote financial inclusion. Stellar's focus on remittance services and cross-border transactions makes it an essential player in the global financial ecosystem.

Stellar's consensus algorithm, the Stellar Consensus Protocol (SCP), enables fast and low-cost transactions, making it an attractive option for users and businesses seeking to move funds across borders efficiently.

Dogecoin, created in 2013 as a lighthearted parody of Bitcoin, has become a community and internet culture symbol. Based on the popular "Doge" meme, Dogecoin features the Shiba Inu dog as its logo and mascot.

Despite its humorous origins, Dogecoin has gained a dedicated community and found use in various charitable initiatives and tipping services on social media platforms. Its simplicity and ease of use have contributed to its enduring popularity.

The cryptocurrency landscape is a diverse and dynamic ecosystem, with many notable cryptocurrencies each contributing unique features, use cases, and innovations. From privacy-focused coins like Monero to blockchain interoperability projects like Polkadot and decentralized finance platforms like Uniswap, these cryptocurrencies are driving the ongoing transformation of the global financial system and beyond.

The potential influence of these well-known cryptocurrencies on banking, government, and other industries will only grow as blockchain technology advances and gains broader acceptance. This will bring in a new era of decentralization, trustless interactions, and financial freedom.

CHAPTER V

Investing in Cryptocurrencies

Understanding Market Volatility

The market volatility and sharp price swings of cryptocurrency marketplaces are well-known. The lack of comprehensive regulation, speculative trading, and market sentiment significantly drive these price swings. Additionally, cryptocurrencies' relatively small market size compared to traditional financial markets makes them susceptible to larger price movements triggered by substantial buy or sell orders. Unlike traditional assets, cryptocurrencies lack intrinsic value, leading to more speculative valuation methods and amplified volatility. Moreover, technological developments, regulatory changes, and media coverage significantly impact market sentiment and drive price movements.

The introduction or anticipation of new regulations can have a profound impact on cryptocurrency prices. Positive regulatory developments boost investor confidence, leading to price surges, while negative news or crackdowns can cause sharp price drops. The lack of regulation also makes the cryptocurrency market vulnerable to price manipulation. Market participants can engage in pump-and-dump schemes, artificially inflating prices and selling for profit, leading to sudden spikes and crashes.

Announcements of technological upgrades or protocol changes can cause significant price movements in cryptocurrencies. Investors react positively to scalability, speed, and security improvements, driving up prices.

Conversely, negative news, security breaches, or hacks can lead to fear and uncertainty, resulting in price declines. Media coverage plays a crucial role in driving market sentiment. Positive news stories, endorsements, or institutional adoption can create optimism, leading to price rallies, while negative news can result in fear and selling pressure.

Cryptocurrency market volatility offers opportunities for significant profits but also exposes investors to substantial risks. Short-term traders can capitalize on rapid price swings for quick gains, while long-term investors can buy during market dips and hold for potential long-term growth. However, emotional decision-making during periods of high volatility can lead to hasty and uninformed trading, resulting in unfavorable outcomes.

Market volatility can impact the adoption of cryptocurrencies as a means of payment or a store of value. Frequent and unpredictable price fluctuations can deter businesses from accepting cryptocurrencies, as they may not want to risk receiving payments that could dramatically decrease in value shortly after. For users, volatility can also be a deterrent to using cryptocurrencies for day-to-day transactions. The fear of losing value due to price swings can lead to a preference for stable currencies or traditional payment methods.

Risk management strategies are crucial for investors in the face of market volatility. Diversification, spreading investments across different cryptocurrencies and traditional assets, can help reduce exposure to any single asset's price fluctuations. Setting stop-loss orders and profit-taking levels can protect against substantial losses or secure gains during times of rapid price movements. Moreover, employing a long-term investment strategy and avoiding emotional decision-making can help weather short-term market turbulence.

In conclusion, market volatility is an inherent characteristic of cryptocurrency, driven by factors such as regulatory developments, market sentiment, technological advancements, and market manipulation. While volatility offers profit opportunities, it also exposes investors to significant risks. Understanding the causes and effects of market volatility is crucial for investors seeking to navigate this dynamic and fast-paced environment successfully. Employing risk management strategies, conducting fundamental analysis, staying informed, and adopting a long-term investment approach can help mitigate risks and take advantage of the opportunities presented by cryptocurrency market volatility.

As the cryptocurrency market matures and gains wider acceptance, market volatility may gradually subside, making it a more stable and reliable asset class. Until then, navigating the highs and lows of the cryptocurrency market requires diligence, adaptability, and a keen understanding of market dynamics.

Assessing Risk and Reward

Investing in cryptocurrencies has become a popular pursuit, with the allure of potential high returns attracting investors from all walks of life. However, the volatile nature of the cryptocurrency market demands a thorough assessment of risk and reward to make informed investment decisions. Market volatility is a significant risk factor in cryptocurrency investments. The extreme price fluctuations driven by market sentiment, regulatory developments, technological advancements, and speculative trading can lead to significant short-term gains or losses. Additionally, the lack of comprehensive regulation in cryptocurrency creates uncertainty and potential legal risks for investors, as regulatory changes or crackdowns in different jurisdictions can impact market dynamics.

Security risks are another crucial aspect to consider. Cryptocurrency exchanges and wallets are susceptible to security breaches and hacking attacks, potentially losing invested funds. Liquidity risks are also prevalent, as some cryptocurrencies may suffer from low liquidity, making it challenging to execute trades without significantly affecting prices. To mitigate risks, diversification is often recommended. Spreading investments across multiple cryptocurrencies can help reduce exposure to any single asset's price fluctuations and improve overall portfolio stability.

Conducting fundamental analysis is essential for understanding the long-term potential of cryptocurrency projects. Assessing the technology, development progress, team expertise, real-world use cases, and community support can differentiate between solid investments and speculative assets. Additionally, technical analysis, which involves studying historical price and trading volume data to determine patterns and trends, can provide insights into trades' potential entry and exit points.

Evaluating the potential rewards in cryptocurrency investments is equally important. Cryptocurrencies have historically offered higher returns than traditional asset classes, attracting investors seeking significant profits. Early adoption benefits are also a consideration, as investing in promising projects during their early stages can lead to substantial growth and long-term value appreciation.

However, investing in cryptocurrencies is not without its challenges. Market manipulation is a risk in the largely unregulated cryptocurrency space. Manipulative practices, such as pump-and-dump schemes, can lead to significant price swings and result in substantial losses for investors. Moreover, the evolving regulatory landscape poses uncertainty for investors, as changes in regulations can impact market sentiment and influence investment decisions.

Technological risks are also relevant. Cryptocurrency projects face challenges in delivering on their technological promises. Network vulnerabilities, coding errors, and scalability issues can impact a project's long-term viability and success.

Despite these challenges, some investors view cryptocurrencies as an inflation hedge. Cryptocurrencies like Bitcoin, with their capped supply and scarcity, are considered a store of value during periods of economic uncertainty or inflationary pressures.

As the cryptocurrency market evolves, so do the long-term considerations for investors. The market's relative youth and evolving nature may lead to decreased volatility and increased investor confidence over time. However, investors must remain vigilant, continually update their risk assessment strategies, and stay informed about regulatory developments and technological advancements in cryptocurrency.

In conclusion, assessing risk and reward in investing in cryptocurrencies is a complex process that demands comprehensive analysis and a balanced approach. Market volatility, security risks, regulatory uncertainty, technological challenges, and potential rewards are all factors that need careful consideration. By implementing risk management strategies, conducting thorough analysis, and staying informed, investors can confidently navigate the cryptocurrency market and achieve their investment objectives in this transformative and dynamic financial landscape.

Choosing the Right Exchange

As cryptocurrencies continue to gain mainstream attention, more investors are venturing into the digital asset space. One critical aspect of cryptocurrency investing is selecting the right exchange platform to facilitate the buying, selling, and trading of these digital assets. With numerous exchanges available, each offering unique features and services, choosing the right one can be daunting.

When choosing a cryptocurrency exchange, several factors need to be considered. The security and reputation of an exchange should be the top priority for any investor. Researching the exchange's security measures, such as cold storage for funds and two-factor authentication (2FA) for user accounts, is essential. Additionally, considering the exchange's reputation and user reviews can provide insights into its track record and reliability.

Another crucial factor is regulatory compliance. Choosing a regulated exchange ensures that the platform adheres to applicable laws and regulations, enhancing investor protection and trust. Checking for licensing and compliance with financial authorities can help ensure a safe trading environment.

The selection of available cryptocurrencies is also an important consideration. Different exchanges offer varying selections of cryptocurrencies. Investors should choose an exchange that supports the digital assets they intend to trade or invest in.

Trading fees can significantly impact investment returns, so evaluating fee structures is crucial. Investors should be aware of the trading fees, withdrawal fees, and deposit fees charged by the exchange to optimize their trading strategies.

A user-friendly interface is vital for an enjoyable trading experience. A well-designed exchange can save time and effort, especially for beginner investors who may not be familiar with complex trading interfaces.

Liquidity is another crucial aspect to consider. The ease of purchasing and selling assets on an exchange is referred to as liquidity. Choosing an exchange with sufficient liquidity ensures that orders can be executed promptly and at fair market prices.

In terms of risks, centralized exchanges (CEX) are the most common type of exchange. While they offer convenience and a wide range of trading pairs, they pose security risks. If an exchange's security measures are breached, user funds can be at risk of theft. Additionally, centralized control introduces a single point of failure, making CEXs vulnerable to hacking attacks and potential internal fraud.

Decentralized exchanges (DEX) operate on blockchain networks, allowing peer-to-peer trading without the need for intermediaries. DEXs offer greater security and user privacy since funds remain in users' control during transactions. However, DEXs may have limited liquidity and a narrower selection of cryptocurrencies compared to CEXs. Moreover, the user experience can be less intuitive for those not familiar with decentralized protocols.

Hybrid exchanges aim to combine the benefits of centralized and decentralized platforms. They may offer secure and non-custodial trading services, allowing users to control their funds during transactions. While hybrid exchanges address some concerns related to security and control, users must still consider the platform's overall security measures and compliance with regulations.

Investors should follow best practices to ensure a secure and seamless trading experience. Conducting thorough research on exchanges is crucial before making a decision. Investors can make informed choices by researching an exchange's security measures, reputation, regulatory compliance, and available services.

Implementing strong security measures is essential for safeguarding personal data and digital assets. Enabling two-factor authentication (2FA) for exchange accounts and using secure passwords are simple but effective security practices. Additionally, considering the use of hardware wallets for long-term storage of cryptocurrencies can reduce exposure to potential security breaches.

Diversification is key to managing risk. Spreading investments across different cryptocurrencies and exchanges helps reduce risk exposure to any single asset or platform. This approach ensures that potential losses from a single investment do not significantly impact an investor's overall portfolio.

Investors should start small and test the platform when using a new exchange. Making small transactions initially allows investors to assess the platform's performance and security before committing significant funds.

Staying informed about exchange news and updates is crucial for making informed decisions. Awareness of changes in an exchange's terms of service, fees, or regulations can help investors adapt their trading strategies accordingly.

Finally, withdrawing funds to a secure wallet when not actively trading is essential for security reasons. Keeping a significant portion of funds on an exchange increases the risk of loss in the event of a security breach.

In conclusion, selecting the best cryptocurrency exchange is essential to starting a profitable investment adventure in the realm of digital assets. The security of user funds and regulatory compliance are paramount considerations when selecting an exchange. Evaluating available cryptocurrencies, trading fees, user interface, and liquidity can help investors find an exchange that aligns with their needs and preferences.

Investors should know the risks associated with different exchange types, such as centralized exchanges with their security vulnerabilities and decentralized exchanges with limited liquidity. Hybrid exchanges offer a balance between security and user experience.

Investors can make knowledgeable decisions and mitigate risks by conducting thorough research, implementing strong security measures, and diversifying assets and exchanges. Staying informed about exchange news and adhering to best practices ensures a secure and seamless trading experience.

Choosing the right exchange is a crucial step toward a successful cryptocurrency investment journey. By carefully evaluating options, understanding the risks, and adhering to best practices, investors can confidently navigate the cryptocurrency market and optimize their investment strategies in this dynamic and rapidly evolving digital landscape.

Creating a Cryptocurrency Portfolio

As cryptocurrencies continue to disrupt traditional finance, investors increasingly seek to capitalize on the potential for significant returns in this emerging asset class. One of the fundamental aspects of successful cryptocurrency investing is creating a well-structured and balanced portfolio. A carefully constructed cryptocurrency portfolio can help manage risk, optimize returns, and navigate the volatile market dynamics.

By distributing investments over several assets, diversification serves as a risk management strategy that lessens exposure to asset price volatility. Cryptocurrencies are known for their inherent market volatility, and diversification can help mitigate potential losses in case of a market downturn in a specific cryptocurrency. Additionally, diversification allows investors to participate in various cryptocurrency markets while reducing dependency on any single asset's performance.

Creating a cryptocurrency portfolio involves assessing risk tolerance and investment goals. Understanding personal risk tolerance and investment objectives helps shape the portfolio's composition. Thorough fundamental analysis is also necessary before including a cryptocurrency in the portfolio. Evaluating the technology, development team, real-world use cases, and community support can help identify fundamentally strong projects.

Market capitalization and liquidity are vital factors to consider when constructing a portfolio. Larger cryptocurrencies with higher liquidity are generally less susceptible to extreme price fluctuations, making them suitable for core holdings in the portfolio. Determining the allocation of funds to different cryptocurrencies is a critical step in portfolio construction. Investors may allocate a higher percentage of funds to established cryptocurrencies with proven track records, while allocating a smaller percentage to riskier assets with higher growth potential.

The core and satellite approach is a popular portfolio strategy. It involves creating a core portfolio of well-established cryptocurrencies with strong fundamentals. Surrounding the core, satellite positions comprise smaller allocations to riskier assets offering higher growth potential. This strategy seeks to balance stability with opportunities for significant returns.

Another portfolio strategy is market capitalization-based allocation. This approach involves distributing funds based on the market capitalization of cryptocurrencies. Investors allocate more funds to cryptocurrencies with higher market capitalization, considering them more stable and less prone to extreme price movements.

Sector-based diversification is another approach. It involves allocating funds across different cryptocurrency sectors or use cases. For example, investors may include cryptocurrencies focused on decentralized finance (DeFi), non-fungible tokens (NFTs), or privacy coins. Sector-based diversification allows exposure to multiple emerging trends in the cryptocurrency space.

To manage risk in cryptocurrency portfolios, several techniques can be employed. Rebalancing is one such strategy that involves adjusting the portfolio's allocation periodically to maintain the desired risk-return profile. As cryptocurrencies' prices fluctuate, the portfolio's composition may deviate from the initial allocation. Rebalancing helps align the portfolio with the investor's risk tolerance and investment goals.

Dollar-cost averaging (DCA) is another risk management technique. It involves investing fixed funds at regular intervals, regardless of the cryptocurrency's price. By using this method, investors might potentially lessen the impact of short-term price volatility by purchasing more cryptocurrency units during periods of low price and less units during periods of high price.

Implementing stop-loss orders can protect against significant losses during market downturns. A stop-loss order triggers a market sell order when the price of a cryptocurrency falls to a predetermined level, limiting potential losses.

In conclusion, building a cryptocurrency portfolio is a dynamic process that necessitates giving numerous elements considerable thought. A key idea in risk management and return optimization is diversification.

Investing in a variety of cryptocurrencies allows investors to take advantage of market opportunities while lowering their reliance on the performance of any one asset.

Key considerations in portfolio construction include risk tolerance, investment goals, project fundamentals, market capitalization, and liquidity. Assessing these factors helps investors determine the appropriate asset allocation and portfolio weighting.

Cryptocurrency portfolio strategies, such as the core and satellite approach, market capitalization-based allocation, and sector-based diversification, provide different approaches to achieving portfolio balance. Implementing risk management techniques, such as rebalancing, dollar-cost averaging, and stop-loss orders, further enhances portfolio stability and helps investors navigate market volatility.

Constructing a cryptocurrency portfolio requires a thoughtful approach, ongoing monitoring, and adaptability to market dynamics. By understanding risk management strategies and adopting diversification techniques, investors can make informed and successful investment decisions in the dynamic and transformative world of cryptocurrencies.

CHAPTER VI

Storing Cryptocurrencies Securely

Cryptocurrency Wallets Overview

In the fast-paced world of cryptocurrencies, the safe storage and management of digital assets are crucial for investors and users alike. Cryptocurrency wallets are vital in securing and accessing cryptocurrencies, making them essential to the blockchain ecosystem.

A cryptocurrency wallet is a digital tool allowing users to store, receive, and send digital currencies securely. Contrary to physical wallets holding traditional currencies, cryptocurrency wallets store private keys required to access and transfer cryptocurrencies on the blockchain. Private keys are cryptographic keys that provide ownership and control over digital assets, emphasizing the critical role of wallets in protecting users' funds. Security is paramount when dealing with cryptocurrencies, and cryptocurrency wallets offer various features to safeguard users' digital assets. They generate and manage both public and private keys. Public keys serve as the wallet address, allowing users to receive digital assets. On the other hand, private keys grant access to the stored cryptocurrencies and must be kept secret to prevent unauthorized access.

Many cryptocurrency wallets use seed phrases or mnemonic phrases to back up and recover wallets. These phrases consist of a series of randomly produced words that act as a backup for the wallet's private keys. Writing down and storing the seed phrase securely is essential if the wallet is lost or inaccessible.

Hardware wallets are tangible objects made specifically for offline private key storage. From the fact that the private keys are kept off the internet, they provide a high degree of security. Hardware wallets are said to be among the most secure methods for keeping cryptocurrency. Software wallets, on the other hand, are installed apps or software programs on PCs, smartphones, and other devices. They can be divided into two more categories: desktop and mobile wallets. Desktop wallets are installed on personal computers and provide access to private keys locally. They offer more security compared to online wallets. On the other hand, mobile wallets are installed on smartphones and offer convenience for users who need to access their cryptocurrencies on the go.

Online wallets, or web wallets, are hosted on web-based platforms and can be accessed through internet browsers. While they offer convenience, online wallets are more susceptible to security risks due to the exposure of private keys to the internet. Paper wallets involve printing the wallet's public and private keys on physical paper. This method keeps private keys entirely offline, making it a secure option for long-term storage. However, users must keep the paper wallet safe from damage and unauthorized access.

Creating backups of your wallet, particularly seed phrases, is critical in case of device loss or failure. Storing multiple backups in secure and separate locations is recommended. Regularly updating your wallet software helps protect against potential vulnerabilities and ensures you have access to the latest security features.

Using strong passwords and enabling multi-factor authentication (MFA) adds a further degree of security to your wallet, safeguarding against unauthorized access. Be cautious of phishing attempts, where malicious actors try to steal your private information through deceptive emails or websites. Always ensure you are using official wallet applications and websites.

When making a transaction to a new wallet or exchange, test with a small amount first to ensure the transaction is successful prior to sending larger amounts. For long-term storage of significant amounts of cryptocurrencies, consider using hardware wallets, which offer enhanced security by keeping private keys offline.

In conclusion, cryptocurrency wallets are essential for securing and managing digital assets. Understanding the security features, types of wallets, and best practices is crucial for guaranteeing the safety of cryptocurrency holdings. The highest level of security is provided by hardware wallets, while software wallets provide convenience for regular transactions.

Regardless of the wallet type, backing up your wallet securely, keeping software updated, implementing strong passwords and MFA, being cautious of phishing attempts, and testing transactions with small amounts are all fundamental practices for managing cryptocurrencies safely.

As the cryptocurrency space continues to evolve, developing new wallet solutions and security features will significantly enhance user experience and protect users' funds. Cryptocurrency users can confidently and securely engage in this transformative financial ecosystem by staying informed and adopting best practices.

Types of Wallets (Hardware, Software, Paper)

As cryptocurrencies gain mainstream adoption, the need for secure and reliable storage solutions becomes paramount. Cryptocurrency wallets are essential for managing digital assets, allowing users to securely store, receive, and send cryptocurrencies. These wallets come in various forms, each offering distinct features and levels of security. This section will explore the different types of cryptocurrency wallets, including hardware wallets, software wallets, and paper wallets. By understanding the characteristics and functionalities of each type, users can make informed decisions about the most suitable wallet for their needs.

Hardware wallets are tangible objects designed specifically for the secure storage of cryptocurrencies. By keeping private keys offline and out of the reach of possible online attackers, their offline approach adds an extra degree of security. The most common hardware wallets come in the form of USB-like devices equipped with buttons for navigating the user interface. When a user wants to make a transaction, the hardware wallet generates the transaction details, which are signed within the device. This process ensures that the private keys never leave the secure environment of the hardware wallet, reducing the risk of potential hacks or unauthorized access.

The main advantage of hardware wallets lies in their immunity to malware or phishing attacks. Since private keys are kept offline, they are less susceptible to being compromised by malicious software or phishing attempts. Additionally, the use of Hardware Security Modules (HSMs) in many hardware wallets further enhances their security. HSMs are specialized cryptographic devices that securely manage private keys and perform cryptographic operations, adding an extra layer of protection against attacks.

Hardware wallets are also user-friendly, often featuring a simple user interface that is straightforward to navigate, making them accessible even to less tech-savvy individuals. However, hardware wallets come at a cost, with prices varying depending on the brand and model.

The investment in a hardware wallet is justified by the added security and peace of mind it provides to users with substantial cryptocurrency holdings or those seeking the utmost security for their digital assets.

Software wallets are digital applications or programs that users install on their devices, such as computers, smartphones, or tablets. They are widely available and offer a range of options to store, send, and receive cryptocurrencies. Software wallets can be further categorized into desktop wallets and mobile wallets.

Desktop wallets are applications installed on personal computers or laptops. They give users full control over their private keys, allowing them to manage their cryptocurrencies directly from their computers. Desktop wallets can be further subdivided into full-node wallets, light wallets, and multi-coin wallets.

Full-node wallets download and store the entire blockchain, making them robust and secure but requiring significant storage space and bandwidth. Light wallets, or SPV (Simplified Payment Verification) wallets, do not download the entire blockchain. Instead, they retrieve necessary transaction data from other full nodes, offering a more lightweight option that requires less storage space and bandwidth. Multi-coin wallets support multiple cryptocurrencies, allowing users to manage different assets within a single application.

Desktop wallets provide a secure and convenient balance. By keeping their private keys on their own devices, users can reduce their dependency on outside parties and keep control of their funds. However, desktop wallets require users to take responsibility for their device's security, ensuring they have robust antivirus software and keep their operating systems up to date.

Applications for smartphones and tablets called mobile wallets provide easy access to cryptocurrencies while on the go. They are prevalent among users who frequently make transactions or need quick access to their digital assets. Mobile wallets provide a user-friendly interface, making them accessible to a broader audience.

Mobile wallets also come in various forms, including single-currency wallets and multi-currency wallets. Single-currency wallets are designed to support a specific cryptocurrency, while multi-currency wallets offer compatibility with different digital assets. As with desktop wallets, mobile wallet users should take precautions to ensure the security of their devices and avoid downloading unknown or unverified applications.
Paper wallets offer an alternative method of securely storing cryptocurrencies. They involve printing the wallet's public and private keys on a physical piece of paper. Since the keys are entirely offline, paper wallets are considered cold storage solutions, making them resistant to online threats. Paper wallets are often generated through websites or applications allowing users to create and print them for safekeeping.
Creating a paper wallet involves generating a new wallet address and its corresponding private key. Users should ensure that they generate the paper wallet on a secure and offline device to avoid potential private key exposure. Once the paper wallet is printed, it should be stored securely and protected from damage or unauthorized access.

Paper wallets offer simplicity and cost-effectiveness, as they do not need any additional hardware or software. However, paper wallets also come with some inherent risks. Since the private key is physically printed, it can be susceptible to loss, damage, or theft. Therefore, users must take extra precautions to store the paper wallet securely, such as using fireproof safes or safety deposit boxes.

Cryptocurrency wallets are essential tools for managing digital assets securely. Users have various options to choose from, each offering different levels of security and accessibility. The highest level of security is provided by hardware wallets, which store private keys offline and are resistant to online attacks. They are ideal for users with substantial cryptocurrency holdings or those seeking the utmost security.

Software wallets, including desktop and mobile wallets, balance security and accessibility. They allow users to manage their cryptocurrencies on their devices while requiring them to take responsibility for their device's security. Software wallets are suitable for users who frequently make transactions and need quick access to their digital assets.

Paper wallets provide an alternative cold storage solution, allowing users to generate and print wallet addresses and private keys on a tangible piece of paper. While cost-effective and straightforward, paper wallets risk physical damage, loss, or theft.

Ultimately, the choice of wallet type depends on individual preferences, risk tolerance, and the amount of cryptocurrency being managed. Regardless of the wallet type, users should prioritize security by implementing best practices, such as enabling multi-factor authentication, keeping software up to date, and storing backup phrases securely. With a comprehensive understanding of the different wallet types and their features, users can confidently store, manage, and transact with cryptocurrencies while ensuring the safety and security of their digital assets.

Best Practices for Securing Your Wallet

The financial landscape has completely changed as a result of the rise of cryptocurrencies, giving people unprecedented ownership over their digital assets. As the adoption of cryptocurrencies grows, so does the need for robust security measures to protect these valuable holdings. Cryptocurrency wallets are at the heart of this security, serving as the gateway to managing and safeguarding digital assets. In this section, we will explore the best practices for securing your wallet, focusing on essential steps to protect against potential threats, prevent unauthorized access, and ensure the safety of your cryptocurrency holdings.

The first step in securing your cryptocurrency is selecting a secure wallet. Hardware wallets, such as Ledger and Trezor, are considered the gold standard for security. These tangible devices keep your private keys offline, reducing the risk of exposure to online threats. Hardware wallets often use Hardware Security Modules (HSMs) to provide additional protection. Software wallets, including desktop and mobile wallets, are also viable options, but they require users to take extra precautions to guarantee their devices are free from malware and security vulnerabilities. Researching and choosing reputable wallet providers with a track record of security and user trust is essential.

Multi-factor authentication (MFA) is a vital security feature that gives your wallet an additional degree of protection. Before being able to access the wallet, MFA requires users to supply extra information, typically in the form of a one-time code texted to their mobile device. Even in the event that someone manages to get their hands on your password, the risk of illegal access is greatly decreased with two-factor authentication (2FA) or biometric verification. Many cryptocurrency wallet providers offer MFA options, and users should take advantage of this feature to enhance the security of their accounts.

Creating strong and unique passwords for your cryptocurrency wallets is essential. Avoid using easily guessable passwords or common phrases that could be vulnerable to brute-force attacks. A strong password should combine uppercase and lowercase letters, numbers, and special characters. Furthermore, avoid using the same password for many accounts, as this raises the possibility of a breach of security in the event that one account is compromised.

Backup phrases or seed phrases are crucial for wallet recovery in case of device loss, damage, or theft. These phrases consist of a series of words that act as a backup for your wallet's private keys. It is essential to write down these phrases on physical paper and store them securely in a location known only to you. Avoid storing backup phrases digitally or on cloud storage, as these methods can be susceptible to hacking or unauthorized access. Treat your backup phrases as you would treat cash or valuable possessions, keeping them safe from prying eyes and potential threats.

Updating the software in your wallet is an essential security precaution. Bug fixes, security patches, and enhancements that address possible vulnerabilities are frequently included in software upgrades. Older software puts your wallet at risk of security breaches and increases its vulnerability to hacking attempts. Keep an eye out for updates and employ them right away to keep your wallet current and safe.

Phishing attempts are common in cryptocurrency, with malicious actors attempting to steal sensitive information by posing as legitimate entities through deceptive emails or websites. Always verify the authenticity of any wallet-related communications and avoid from clicking on suspicious links or providing personal information without thorough verification. Official wallet providers will never ask for your private keys or backup phrases via email or other unsecured channels.

Before making significant transactions, consider testing your wallet with a small amount of cryptocurrency. This practice helps ensure that your wallet functions correctly, and you are comfortable with the transaction process. If any issues arise, you can solve them before dealing with more substantial amounts, minimizing potential risks and errors.

The security of your cryptocurrency wallet extends beyond the wallet itself to the devices you use to access it. Make sure that your smartphone, computer, or tablet has updated antivirus and anti-malware software to protect against potential threats. Avoid using public Wi-Fi networks or insecure connections when accessing your wallet, as these networks can be vulnerable to hacking attempts.

Cold storage solutions involve storing your private keys offline, away from internet-connected devices. Hardware and paper wallets are instances of cold storage solutions. Keeping your private keys offline minimizes the risk of cyberattacks and online theft. Cold storage is highly recommended for long-term storage of significant amounts of cryptocurrencies as an additional security measure.

The cryptocurrency landscape constantly evolves, and new security threats may emerge. Staying vigilant and educating yourself about the latest security practices is crucial for safeguarding your digital assets. Regularly reading security-related articles, staying informed about potential vulnerabilities, and being aware of common scams can help you identify and mitigate risks effectively.

Securing your cryptocurrency wallet is of utmost importance in digital assets' dynamic and fast-paced world. By adhering to best practices such as choosing a secure wallet, enabling multi-factor authentication, using strong passwords, and storing backup phrases securely, users can significantly mitigate the risk of illegal access and potential theft. Regularly updating wallet software, being cautious of phishing attempts, and testing transactions with small amounts are further steps to guarantee the safety of your digital assets.

Implementing cold storage solutions, remaining vigilant, and staying educated about the latest security trends are vital components of a comprehensive security strategy. Being a responsible and secure participant in the blockchain ecosystem requires you to take proactive steps to protect your digital assets as the use of cryptocurrencies grows. By following these best practices, users can confidently navigate the cryptocurrency landscape and maintain the integrity of their digital wealth.

CHAPTER VII

Cryptocurrency Trading Strategies

Day Trading vs. Long-Term Investing

The cryptocurrency market has witnessed exponential growth, attracting many investors seeking to capitalize on its potential for significant returns. The two most common approaches taken by cryptocurrency investors are long-term and day trading. Purchasing and selling cryptocurrencies in a single day is known as day trading, but long-term investing means keeping assets for a long time—often years. The main distinctions, advantages, and risks between day trading and long-term cryptocurrency investment will be examined in this section, enabling investors to make well-informed choices depending on their risk tolerance and financial objectives.

Buying and selling cryptocurrencies on the same day is known as day trading, and it's a short-term investment strategy. By using market volatility, day traders seek to make profit on intraday price swings. High levels of technical analysis proficiency, market awareness, and decision-making agility are necessary for this approach. Leverage is a common tool used by day traders to improve the size of their winnings. This can increase returns but also raises the possibility of suffering big losses.

One of the primary advantages of day trading is the potential for quick profits. Since day traders execute multiple trades throughout the day, they can capitalize on even minor price fluctuations to generate returns. Additionally, day traders are not exposed to the long-term price fluctuations of cryptocurrencies, reducing their exposure to potential market downturns.

However, day trading is a high-stress and demanding strategy that requires constant market monitoring. Traders must be disciplined and emotionally detached from their investments, as making impulsive decisions based on emotions can lead to losses. Furthermore, day trading is unsuitable for inexperienced investors, as it involves significant risk and complexity.

Long-term investing, also known as HODLing (a term derived from "hold" in cryptocurrency circles), involves buying and holding cryptocurrencies for an extended period. Long-term investors believe in the long-term potential of the asset and are less concerned about short-term price fluctuations. Patience and a firm belief in the underlying technology and use case of cryptocurrencies are necessary for this approach.

The possibility of large gains in wealth over time is one of the main advantages of long-term investing. Over time, cryptocurrencies have grown remarkably, with some assets seeing exponential price gains. Successful initiatives can generate long-term value, which investors can profit from by holding onto assets for a longer time.

Long-term investing is also less time-consuming and less stressful compared to day trading. Investors do not need to monitor the market or execute frequent trades constantly. People who have a lengthy investing horizon and a low tolerance for market volatility should use this strategy in particular.

But investing for the long run is not without risks. The price of cryptocurrencies can fluctuate sharply over time, and the markets can be very volatile. Investors may need to endure periods of market downturns, and some cryptocurrencies may fail or become obsolete over time.

Both day trading and long-term investing carry inherent risks due to the cryptocurrency market's volatility. Day traders are exposed to significant price fluctuations within a single trading day, amplifying the potential for both gains and losses. Using leverage in day trading can also increase risk exposure, leading to substantial losses if trades go against the trader's expectations.

On the other hand, long-term investors are exposed to market volatility over an extended period. While they may benefit from the long-term growth potential of cryptocurrencies, they must also endure market downturns and fluctuations. It is essential for long-term investors to have a strong belief in the fundamentals of the cryptocurrencies they hold and to be prepared for potential market corrections.

Day trading and long-term investing also differ in their tax implications. Day trading may result in more frequent taxable events, as each trade is considered taxable. This means day traders may need to keep track of more transactions for tax reporting purposes, potentially adding complexity to their tax filings.

Long-term investing, on the other hand, may result in fewer taxable events since investors hold onto assets for an extended period. Depending on the tax jurisdiction, long-term capital gains tax rates may also be more favorable compared to short-term capital gains rates for day trading.

The emotional aspect of trading is significant in both day trading and long-term investing. Day traders must remain calm and disciplined, avoiding emotional decisions driven by fear or greed. The high-stress nature of day trading can lead to emotional burnout if not managed effectively.

In contrast, long-term investors must maintain conviction in their investment thesis, especially during market downturns. The temptation to sell during bear markets can be strong, but successful long-term investors understand the importance of staying committed to their long-term goals.

Day trading requires a substantial time commitment, as traders must actively monitor the market and execute trades throughout the day. This can be challenging for individuals with other professional or personal commitments.

Long-term investing, on the other hand, requires less time and effort, as investors can adopt a "buy and hold" approach. Long-term investors can focus on conducting research and due diligence when initially selecting cryptocurrencies to invest in and periodically reassessing their investment thesis.

Day trading and long-term investing may also be subject to different regulatory considerations. Day traders may be subject to special laws or licensing requirements in some jurisdictions; breaking these rules may have legal repercussions.

Long-term investing may not face the same level of regulatory scrutiny, but investors should still stay informed about the evolving regulatory landscape for cryptocurrencies in their respective jurisdictions.

Diversification is a crucial consideration for both day traders and long-term investors. Day traders may diversify their portfolios by trading multiple cryptocurrencies or utilizing different trading strategies to spread risk.

Long-term investors can also benefit from diversification by holding a diversified portfolio of cryptocurrencies. Diversification can help mitigate risk by reducing exposure to any single cryptocurrency's price fluctuations. Long-term investors may also consider including traditional assets, such as stocks or bonds, in their portfolio for added diversification.

Day trading and long-term investing are two distinct strategies in the cryptocurrency market, each catering to different investor profiles and financial goals. Day trading provides the potential for quick profits but requires a high level of skill, discipline, and emotional detachment. Long-term investing, on the other hand, emphasizes patience and conviction in the long-term potential of cryptocurrencies.

Both strategies carry inherent risks due to the volatility of the cryptocurrency market. Investors should carefully assess their risk tolerance, financial goals, and time commitment before choosing a strategy. Diversification and adherence to best practices, such as secure wallet management and risk management, are essential regardless of the chosen strategy.

Ultimately, the decision between day trading and long-term investing should be based on individual preferences and circumstances. It is necessary to conduct thorough research, seek advice from financial experts if needed, and stay informed about the evolving dynamics of the cryptocurrency market. By making informed decisions, investors can navigate the cryptocurrency landscape and make strategic choices to achieve their financial objectives.

Technical and Fundamental Analysis

The cryptocurrency market's rapid growth and potential for significant returns have attracted diverse investors seeking profitable opportunities. To make educated decisions in this dynamic landscape, two primary analysis methods come into play: technical analysis and fundamental analysis. Technical analysis involves studying historical price patterns and market trends to predict future price movements, while fundamental analysis evaluates a cryptocurrency's intrinsic value based on its underlying fundamentals. In this section, we will delve into the differences, methodologies, advantages, and limitations of technical and fundamental analysis in cryptocurrency market, empowering investors to make well-rounded decisions tailored to their preferred approach and risk tolerance.

Technical analysis is a method of evaluating cryptocurrency price movements by analyzing historical data and statistical patterns. This approach involves studying chart patterns, trends, and various technical indicators to anticipate future price movements. The foundation of technical analysis lies in the belief that historical price data can offer valuable insights into potential future price movements, allowing investors to execute well-timed buy or sell decisions.

A crucial component of technical analysis is chart patterns, which visually represent historical price movements on cryptocurrency price charts. Common chart patterns entail support and resistance levels, trendlines, and candlestick patterns. Support levels indicate price levels at which a cryptocurrency's price tends to find support, preventing it from declining further. Conversely, resistance levels are price points where a cryptocurrency's price encounters selling pressure, preventing it from rising further.

Technical indicators are mathematical calculations derived from historical price data, helping identify trends, momentum, and potential reversal points in the cryptocurrency market. Traders widely use technical indicators such as Moving Averages (MA), Relative Strength Index (RSI), Moving Average Convergence Divergence (MACD), and Bollinger Bands, among others.

Trends are a basic aspect of technical analysis, reflecting the overall direction of a cryptocurrency's price movement. Trends can be upward (bullish), downward (bearish), or sideways (neutral). Trendlines are graphical representations used to identify trends on price charts, aiding traders in pinpointing potential entry and exit points.

The advantages of technical analysis include its objective approach based on historical data and mathematical calculations. It benefits short-term trading, providing valuable insights into intraday price movements and short-term trends. Moreover, technical analysis is widely used in the cryptocurrency market, with many traders relying on technical indicators to inform their trading decisions.

However, technical analysis has limitations. It relies solely on historical price data, which may not fully account for fundamental developments or events that could significantly impact a cryptocurrency's price. The interpretation of technical indicators can also be subjective, leading to different conclusions among traders. Furthermore, technical analysis does not directly consider market sentiment or external factors influencing cryptocurrency prices.

A technique for determining a cryptocurrency's intrinsic value through an evaluation of its underlying fundamentals is called fundamental analysis. This approach assesses a cryptocurrency's technology, adoption, development team, community support, market demand, and positioning. The fundamental analyst aims to identify overvalued or undervalued cryptocurrencies based on their long-term growth and adoption potential.

A crucial aspect of fundamental analysis is evaluating the technology and development team behind a cryptocurrency project. A strong and innovative technology, backed by a competent and experienced development team, can contribute to a cryptocurrency's long-term success and adoption.

Fundamental analysis also involves assessing cryptocurrency's real-world use case and market demand. A cryptocurrency with a practical application and a strong demand for its services is more likely to have long-term value and growth potential.

The strength of a cryptocurrency's community and network effect is another essential aspect of fundamental analysis. A thriving and engaged community can drive network growth, increase adoption, and create a network effect that attracts more users and investors.

The advantages of fundamental analysis lie in its focus on the long-term potential of cryptocurrencies, making it suitable for investors looking to hold assets for an extended period. It provides a deeper understanding of a cryptocurrency's intrinsic value, helping investors identify potential undervalued assets. Additionally, fundamental analysis considers real-world factors, such as technology, adoption, and market demand, providing a more comprehensive view of a cryptocurrency's potential.

However, fundamental analysis has its limitations. Conducting a thorough fundamental analysis requires significant research and due diligence, which may be time-consuming for investors. Furthermore, while fundamental analysis assesses a cryptocurrency's potential based on its fundamentals, future developments and unexpected events can still impact its price.

Many investors opt to combine both technical and fundamental analysis to make well-rounded investment decisions. Integrating both approaches allows investors to benefit from a more holistic view of the cryptocurrency market.

By combining technical and fundamental analysis, investors can identify confluences, where both approaches support the same investment thesis. For example, if a cryptocurrency exhibits bullish technical signals while also having strong fundamentals and a positive market sentiment, it may indicate a higher probability of a successful investment.

The integration of both technical and fundamental analysis also aids in risk management. Investors can use technical analysis to identify entry and exit points for their investments, while fundamental analysis can help them identify potential risks and opportunities in the long run.

Additionally, investors who utilize both technical and fundamental analysis can be more adaptable in different market conditions. While technical analysis may be more suitable for short-term trading during periods of high volatility, fundamental analysis can guide long-term investment decisions based on a cryptocurrency's potential for growth and adoption.

Technical and fundamental analysis are two distinct methods used to analyze the cryptocurrency market. Technical analysis relies on historical price data and statistical patterns to predict short-term price movements, while fundamental analysis evaluates a cryptocurrency's intrinsic value based on its underlying fundamentals.

When selecting an analysis method, investors should carefully evaluate their financial goals, risk tolerance, as well as investment horizon as each strategy has advantages and disadvantages. Investors can have a more thorough understanding of the cryptocurrency market and make well-informed judgments to effectively traverse the ever-changing and dynamic world of cryptocurrencies by combining technical and fundamental analysis. As the cryptocurrency market continues to mature, both methods will play a significant role in guiding investors' strategies and shaping the future of digital asset investment.

Diversification and Risk Management

With its inherent volatility and potential for substantial gains, the cryptocurrency market has attracted diverse investors seeking lucrative opportunities. However, the unpredictable nature of cryptocurrencies also exposes investors to significant risks. Diversification and risk management are vital components of a strategic approach to investing in cryptocurrencies. In this section, we will explore the concept of diversification, its benefits, and the various methods of risk management that can help investors mitigate potential losses in the cryptocurrency market.

Diversification is a fundamental investment strategy that spreads investments across different assets, industries, or sectors to reduce exposure to any asset's risks. In the context of the cryptocurrency market, diversification can be achieved by holding multiple cryptocurrencies in a portfolio rather than concentrating investments in a single digital asset.

Diversification in cryptocurrency involves spreading investments across various cryptocurrencies with diverse characteristics, use cases, and market positions. By holding a diversified portfolio, investors reduce the risk of significant losses that may occur if a particular cryptocurrency underperforms or faces adverse market conditions. Diversification can also enhance the potential for overall portfolio growth, as gains from well-performing cryptocurrencies can offset losses from others.

The benefits of diversification include risk mitigation, as it helps spread risk across different cryptocurrencies, reducing exposure to any asset's adverse performance. A diversified portfolio can lead to smoother overall portfolio performance, reducing the impact of extreme price swings in any single cryptocurrency. Moreover, diversification allows investors to participate in various market opportunities across different cryptocurrencies and blockchain projects.

Effective risk management is essential to protect capital and reduce potential losses in the highly volatile and speculative cryptocurrency market. Implementing various risk management strategies can help investors navigate the cryptocurrency market's inherent uncertainties and enhance their investment portfolios' long-term stability.

Asset allocation, which divides an investment portfolio among several asset classes, including cryptocurrency, equities, bonds, and commodities, is a crucial risk management technique. Investors can lower the total risk of their portfolio and increase the likelihood of obtaining steady returns, even in the face of fluctuations in individual assets, by diversifying among a variety of asset classes.

The process of routinely modifying an asset allocation in a portfolio to preserve the intended risk-return profile is known as portfolio rebalancing. During market fluctuations, the weightings of different assets in the portfolio may deviate from the initial allocation. Regular rebalancing ensures that the portfolio's risk exposure remains within the defined risk tolerance, aligning with the investor's long-term financial goals.

Stop loss orders are another risk management tool that allows investors to automatically sell a cryptocurrency once its price reaches a predetermined level. These orders help limit potential losses by allowing investors to exit a position before significant losses occur in case of adverse price movements.

Position sizing determines the appropriate amount to invest in each cryptocurrency position within the portfolio.

By applying position sizing techniques, investors can limit the size of individual positions relative to the total portfolio value, reducing the impact of any single asset's adverse performance on the overall portfolio.

Dollar-cost averaging, or DCA, is an investment strategy where investors regularly invest a fixed amount of money into a particular cryptocurrency or portfolio of cryptocurrencies at regular intervals, regardless of market conditions. Through the purchase of more units during periods of low price and fewer units during periods of high price, DCA helps mitigate the overall investment's impact from market volatility.

Setting realistic investment goals is a crucial risk management aspect in cryptocurrency investing. Investors should define clear objectives, time horizons, and risk tolerances aligned with their financial situation and investment objectives. By setting realistic goals, investors can avoid making impulsive decisions driven by emotions during market fluctuations.

Thorough due diligence and research are essential in mitigating risk in the cryptocurrency market. Investors should conduct in-depth analyses of the cryptocurrencies they consider adding to their portfolio. Understanding each cryptocurrency's technology, use case, team, community support, and market dynamics can help investors make well-informed decisions.

Investors in the cryptocurrency market must consider several factors when implementing risk management strategies. First, cryptocurrencies' high volatility and market fluctuations demand that risk management strategies account for sudden price swings. Moreover, the evolving regulatory environment for cryptocurrencies poses regulatory risks that investors must be aware of and adapt to.

Additionally, market liquidity is a crucial consideration in risk management. Some cryptocurrencies may have lower liquidity than others, making it challenging to execute large trades without causing significant price movements. Risk management strategies should consider the liquidity of the cryptocurrencies in the portfolio.

The security of cryptocurrency holdings is another critical risk management consideration. Implementing robust security measures, such as using hardware wallets, multi-factor authentication, and secure password management, can help protect assets from potential hacking and theft.

Finally, psychological factors can significantly impact cryptocurrency investing. Fear of missing out (FOMO) and fear of loss (FOL) can influence investment decisions and lead to impulsive actions. Risk management strategies should account for psychological factors and maintain a disciplined and rational approach to investing. Diversification and risk management are integral components of a strategic approach to investing in the cryptocurrency market. Diversifying across various cryptocurrencies helps mitigate risks associated with individual assets and enhances overall portfolio stability. Implementing multiple risk management strategies, such as asset allocation, portfolio rebalancing, stop loss orders, and dollar-cost averaging, can help investors navigate the inherent uncertainties of the cryptocurrency market and protect their capital from adverse price movements.

Furthermore, considering market volatility, regulatory risks, liquidity, security, and psychological factors is essential in designing effective risk management strategies. As the cryptocurrency market matures and gains mainstream adoption, diversification and risk management will remain fundamental principles in guiding investors toward successful and sustainable cryptocurrency investment strategies. By adopting a disciplined and knowledgeable approach to risk management, investors can position themselves for long-term success in the dynamic and evolving world of cryptocurrencies.

CHAPTER VIII

Regulation and Legal Considerations

Global Cryptocurrency Regulations

Cryptocurrencies have revolutionized the financial landscape, offering decentralized, borderless, and censorship-resistant digital assets. As cryptocurrencies gained popularity, governments and regulators worldwide began to grapple with the need to create appropriate regulatory frameworks to address these digital assets' unique challenges and opportunities. In this section, we will explore the global cryptocurrency regulatory landscape, examining various approaches countries and international bodies take to regulate cryptocurrencies. We will also discuss the impact of regulations on the cryptocurrency market, investor protection, and the future of digital asset innovation.

Cryptocurrencies' decentralized and cross-border nature poses significant challenges for traditional regulatory frameworks. Governments and financial authorities have recognized the importance of creating clear and comprehensive regulations to address various issues related to cryptocurrencies, such as money laundering, terrorist financing, consumer protection, tax evasion, and market manipulation.

Diversification in cryptocurrency involves spreading investments across various cryptocurrencies with diverse characteristics, use cases, and market positions. By holding a diversified portfolio, investors reduce the risk of significant losses that may occur if a particular cryptocurrency underperforms or faces adverse market conditions. Diversification can also enhance the potential for overall portfolio growth, as gains from well-performing cryptocurrencies can offset losses from others.

The benefits of diversification include risk mitigation, as it helps spread risk across different cryptocurrencies, reducing exposure to any asset's adverse performance. A diversified portfolio can lead to smoother overall portfolio performance, reducing the impact of extreme price swings in any single cryptocurrency. Moreover, diversification allows investors to participate in various market opportunities across different cryptocurrencies and blockchain projects.

The approach to cryptocurrency regulations varies significantly from one country to another, reflecting the different legal, economic, and cultural contexts in which these regulations are formulated.

The regulatory approach to cryptocurrencies has evolved over the years in the United States. Securities and Exchange Commission, or SEC, has taken enforcement actions against fraudulent ICOs and unregistered securities offerings. Additionally, the Commodity Futures Trading Commission (CFTC) treats cryptocurrencies as commodities and oversees their trading on futures exchanges. Various states have introduced their own regulations, leading to a patchwork of state-level regulations.

Canada has also taken a proactive approach to cryptocurrency regulations, with its financial regulatory authorities providing clarity on the classification of cryptocurrencies and their taxation.

The European Union (EU) has pursued a harmonized approach to cryptocurrency regulations across its member states. The EU's Fifth Anti-Money Laundering Directive (5AMLD) introduced in 2020 extended AML and KYC requirements to cryptocurrency service providers.

Furthermore, the EU has been investigating the creation of a thorough regulatory framework for cryptocurrencies and blockchain technology.

Asian countries have adopted diverse approaches to cryptocurrency regulations. Japan has taken a progressive stance by recognizing cryptocurrencies as legal payment methods and introducing licensing requirements for cryptocurrency exchanges. South Korea has imposed strict regulations to combat money laundering and protect investors, while China has banned cryptocurrency trading and Initial Coin Offerings.

Countries in the Middle East have shown varying degrees of interest in cryptocurrency regulations. United Arab Emirates and Bahrain have introduced regulations to govern cryptocurrency businesses, while others are still in the early stages of formulating comprehensive frameworks.

Africa has seen a growing interest in cryptocurrencies, but regulatory developments are at an early stage in most countries. Some African nations have issued warnings about the risks of investing in cryptocurrencies, while others are exploring the potential benefits of blockchain technology in various sectors.

The lack of clear and consistent regulations across countries poses challenges for global cryptocurrency businesses and investors. Regulatory uncertainty can hinder innovation and lead to an uneven playing field for cryptocurrency-related startups and enterprises.

Complying with complex and evolving regulations can be costly for cryptocurrency businesses, particularly smaller startups. Compliance costs may act as a barrier to entry, reducing competition and stifling innovation.

The cross-border nature of cryptocurrencies presents challenges for regulators in enforcing local regulations on global cryptocurrency transactions. Regulators are exploring international cooperation to address cross-border regulatory issues.

Strict regulations may discourage innovation and technological development in the cryptocurrency space. Regulatory frameworks that balance consumer protection and innovation are crucial for fostering the industry's growth.

Cryptocurrency regulations can influence public perception and adoption of digital assets. Excessive regulations may discourage potential users from participating in the cryptocurrency market, while supportive regulations can instill confidence and attract more investors.

The global cryptocurrency regulatory landscape is complex and constantly evolving. Governments and regulatory bodies face the challenge of balancing investor protection, risk mitigation, and fostering innovation in cryptocurrency. A diverse range of regulatory approaches is evident across different regions, reflecting countries' varying perspectives and priorities.

As the cryptocurrency market grows and matures, regulators need to adapt their approaches to address emerging challenges and opportunities. Harmonized, clear, and balanced regulations can provide a conducive environment for the responsible growth of the cryptocurrency industry, benefiting investors, businesses, and the broader economy. Collaborative efforts between countries and international bodies will play an important role in shaping the future of cryptocurrency regulations, unlocking the potential of this transformative technology for the global financial ecosystem.

Tax Implications of Cryptocurrency Transactions

The increasing adoption of cryptocurrencies has created new challenges for tax authorities worldwide. As cryptocurrencies gain popularity as a medium of exchange and investment, governments seek to understand and regulate the tax implications of cryptocurrency transactions. In this section, we will explore the tax treatment of cryptocurrencies in different jurisdictions, the challenges faced by taxpayers and tax authorities, and the importance of tax compliance in the evolving landscape of digital assets.

The taxation of cryptocurrencies varies from country to country, with each jurisdiction adopting its approach based on existing tax laws and regulations. While the taxation of cryptocurrencies is still evolving, several key aspects are commonly considered in determining the tax implications of cryptocurrency transactions.

Cryptocurrencies can be classified as either a currency, property, commodity, or security, significantly impacting how they are taxed. Taxable events in cryptocurrency transactions refer to specific actions that trigger tax liabilities, such as selling or exchanging cryptocurrencies for fiat currency or other digital assets, mining activities, and receiving cryptocurrencies as payment for goods or services. Gains from the exchange or sale of cryptocurrencies are liable to capital gains tax in many jurisdictions. The tax rate varies according to the cryptocurrency's classification and the length of time it is held.

The tax treatment of cryptocurrencies varies among countries, with each nation adopting its regulatory approach based on its unique legal and economic considerations.

In the United States, the Internal Revenue Service, or IRS, treats cryptocurrencies as property for tax purposes.

This means capital gains tax applies when cryptocurrencies are sold or exchanged. Additionally, cryptocurrency mined as part of a trade or business is treated as ordinary income.

In the European Union (EU), the tax treatment of cryptocurrencies varies among member states. Some EU countries, like Germany, consider cryptocurrencies as private money and exempt them from value-added tax (VAT). However, capital gains tax may apply to cryptocurrency transactions in some EU countries. Similarly, in the United Kingdom, cryptocurrencies are generally treated as property for tax purposes. Capital gains tax is applicable when cryptocurrencies are sold or exchanged. However, individuals and businesses may also be liable to pay income tax or corporation tax on cryptocurrency-related activities, such as mining and trading.

Australia treats cryptocurrencies as property, subjecting them to capital gains tax. However, if cryptocurrencies are used to pay for goods and services, the transaction is treated as barter, and the goods or services received are subject to goods and services tax (GST).

The taxation of cryptocurrencies presents various challenges for both taxpayers and tax authorities. One vital challenge is the lack of clarity and consistency in cryptocurrency tax regulations. The rapidly evolving nature of cryptocurrencies makes it difficult for tax authorities to formulate clear and uniform tax laws across different jurisdictions. This lack of uniformity can make confusion for taxpayers and businesses operating internationally.

Another challenge is related to reporting and record-keeping. Cryptocurrencies' decentralized and pseudonymous nature makes it challenging for tax authorities to track cryptocurrency transactions. As a result, taxpayers must maintain accurate records of all cryptocurrency-related activities to ensure compliance with tax laws.

It can be difficult to identify the fair market value of cryptocurrencies for taxation reasons, particularly when there is significant price fluctuation. Accurate valuation is crucial for calculating capital gains or losses accurately. Cryptocurrency airdrops and forks, where holders receive new cryptocurrencies without direct purchase, present unique tax challenges. The tax treatment of these events may vary depending on the jurisdiction and the classification of the newly received cryptocurrencies.

Tax compliance in cryptocurrency transactions is crucial for various reasons. Firstly, complying with cryptocurrency tax regulations helps individuals and businesses avoid penalties and legal consequences. Failure to comply with tax laws may result in fines and legal liabilities, which can have severe financial repercussions.

Secondly, tax compliance enhances the reputation and trustworthiness of taxpayers and businesses. Transparent reporting and accurate tax payments demonstrate integrity and responsible citizenship, which can positively affect business relationships and customer trust.

Thirdly, compliant taxpayers play a crucial role in supporting the development of clear and practical tax laws. As the cryptocurrency market evolves, compliant taxpayers' feedback can contribute to formulating effective and fair tax policies.

Maintaining accurate records and complying with tax regulations can help prevent tax audits and inquiries. Being prepared for potential audits reduces stress and ensures a smooth tax reporting process.

Tax authorities are likely to refine their cryptocurrency tax policies as the cryptocurrency market continues to grow and evolve. The appearance of central bank digital currencies, or CBDCs, and stablecoins may further complicate the taxation of cryptocurrencies. Regulators and tax authorities may seek to strike a balance between fostering innovation and ensuring tax compliance in this dynamic sector.

The tax implications of cryptocurrency transactions remain a complex and evolving landscape. Each country grapples with formulating clear and effective tax regulations that balance fostering innovation and ensuring tax compliance. Taxpayers must understand and adhere to the relevant tax laws to avoid possible penalties and legal consequences. Accurate reporting and record-keeping are crucial in navigating the complexities of cryptocurrency taxation.

As the cryptocurrency market grows, tax authorities will likely adapt their approaches to address emerging challenges and trends. Transparent communication between taxpayers, businesses, and regulatory authorities can contribute to the development of pragmatic and effective cryptocurrency tax policies that support innovation, protect investors, and promote a fair and transparent tax system in the digital age.

CHAPTER IX

Cryptocurrency and Blockchain Use Cases

Cryptocurrencies in E-commerce and Retail

The integration of cryptocurrencies into the e-commerce and retail sectors has introduced a new era of innovation, convenience, and financial autonomy. As cryptocurrencies gain popularity as a means of payment and investment, businesses in the e-commerce and retail industries are exploring the benefits of adopting digital assets. In this section, we will delve into the impact of cryptocurrencies on e-commerce and retail, examining the advantages and challenges they bring to businesses and consumers alike.

One of the most significant advantages of using cryptocurrencies in e-commerce and retail is reducing transaction fees. Traditional payment methods, including bank transfers and credit cards, often come with substantial fees, especially for cross-border transactions. Cryptocurrencies allow businesses to bypass intermediaries, lowering transaction costs and increasing profit margins.

Cryptocurrency transactions are processed faster compared to traditional banking systems. With cryptocurrencies, customers can make cross-border payments without the delays associated with currency conversions and international banking protocols. This feature is particularly beneficial for global e-commerce businesses, enabling them to reach a broader customer base more efficiently.

Cryptocurrencies offer enhanced security and privacy in transactions. Blockchain technology, the backbone of most cryptocurrencies, ensures that transactions are recorded tamper-resistant and transparently. Transactions involving cryptocurrencies do not necessitate the sharing of personal information, giving users more privacy and security against identity theft.

By offering those without access to traditional banking systems financial services, cryptocurrencies promote financial inclusion. This is particularly relevant in regions with underdeveloped banking infrastructure, where cryptocurrencies can be more accessible and efficient for financial transactions.

Several major e-commerce platforms and retailers have embraced cryptocurrencies as a payment method. Companies like Overstock, Shopify, and Newegg accept cryptocurrencies as a form of payment for their goods and services. Additionally, some online marketplaces allow merchants to list their products and receive payments in cryptocurrencies, further promoting the adoption of digital assets in e-commerce.

Cryptocurrencies have streamlined cross-border e-commerce transactions, eliminating the complexities associated with traditional banking systems. By accepting cryptocurrencies, businesses can attract international customers and facilitate seamless transactions without the need for currency conversions.

Chargebacks, where customers dispute a transaction and seek a refund from their credit card provider, can be costly for merchants. Cryptocurrency transactions are irreversible, reducing the risk of chargebacks and providing businesses with more secure payment options.

The price volatility of cryptocurrencies remains a significant challenge for businesses and consumers. The fluctuating value of digital assets can lead to potential losses or gains for both buyers and sellers. To address this issue, some e-commerce platforms and retailers offer real-time conversion of cryptocurrencies to fiat currency at the time of purchase.

Although the adoption of cryptocurrencies in e-commerce and retail is growing, it is still relatively limited compared to traditional payment methods. Many consumers are not yet familiar with using cryptocurrencies for online purchases, leading to a lack of trust and hesitancy in adopting this payment method.

Cryptocurrency regulations vary from country to country, leading to regulatory uncertainty for global businesses. Navigating the complex and evolving regulatory landscape poses challenges for e-commerce businesses looking to integrate cryptocurrencies into their payment systems.

To enhance consumer confidence and trust, e-commerce businesses must educate their customers about cryptocurrencies and the benefits they offer. Providing clear and accurate information about cryptocurrency transactions, security features, and potential risks can alleviate consumer concerns and promote adoption.

Implementing secure payment gateways is essential to prioritize security when integrating cryptocurrencies into their payment gateways. Implementing strong security measures, like the two-factor authentication and encryption, can safeguard customer funds and personal information.

Providing reliable customer support for cryptocurrency-related inquiries can help build trust with consumers. Businesses should be prepared to address customer concerns promptly and efficiently to ensure a positive shopping experience.

The increasing interest and adoption of cryptocurrencies in e-commerce and retail suggest that digital assets will likely become more mainstream. As more businesses accept cryptocurrencies, consumer familiarity and confidence in using digital assets for online purchases will likely grow.

Integrating stablecoins, cryptocurrencies pegged to stable assets like fiat currency, offers a potential solution to price volatility concerns. Integrating stablecoins into e-commerce payment systems may give customers a more stable and predictable purchase value.

Cryptocurrencies open up opportunities for businesses to implement innovative loyalty programs and incentives for customers. Using blockchain technology, businesses can create personalized reward systems that offer exclusive benefits and discounts to loyal cryptocurrency users.

Cryptocurrencies have brought transformative changes to the e-commerce and retail sectors, offering numerous advantages for businesses and consumers alike. Lower transaction fees, faster transactions, enhanced security, and financial inclusion are among the key benefits of integrating cryptocurrencies into e-commerce platforms. However, challenges such as price volatility, limited adoption, and regulatory uncertainty must be addressed to fully harness the potential of cryptocurrencies in the e-commerce and retail industries.

To enhance consumer confidence and trust in cryptocurrency transactions, businesses must educate their customers, implement secure payment gateways, and provide reliable customer support. As the adoption of cryptocurrencies grows, businesses can explore innovative loyalty programs and incentives, further promoting the mainstream acceptance of digital assets in the world of e-commerce and retail. Embracing cryptocurrencies offers a path to a more efficient, inclusive, and secure shopping experience, heralding a new era of financial empowerment for businesses and consumers worldwide.

Blockchain in Supply Chain Management

Blockchain technology has disrupted various industries, and one of its most transformative applications is supply chain management. Blockchain's decentralized and immutable nature offers a revolutionary solution to long-standing challenges in supply chain operations, including traceability, transparency, and data integrity. In this section, we will explore the impact of blockchain technology on supply chain management, its advantages, and the challenges it presents to businesses and stakeholders involved in global trade and logistics.

Supply chain management oversees the flow of products and services from the point of origin to the final consumer. It involves multiple stakeholders, including manufacturers, suppliers, distributors, retailers, and logistics providers, working collaboratively to ensure the efficient movement of goods and the delivery of products to end consumers. Supply chain management is critical in business operations, affecting product availability, cost efficiency, customer satisfaction, and overall competitiveness in the marketplace. However, traditional supply chain practices have been burdened by inefficiencies, lack of transparency, and susceptibility to fraud and counterfeit products.

A form of distributed ledger technology called blockchain keeps an open, transparent, and decentralized record of all transactions made via a network of computers. An unchangeable chain of blocks is created when every transaction, or "block," is cryptographically connected to the one before it. Every link in the supply chain has access to a single source of truth due to this distributed, impenetrable ledger. Transparency and traceability are two major benefits of implementing blockchain in supply chain management. A comprehensive and auditable history of the product's path through the supply chain is provided by the ability to track every transaction made on the blockchain back to its original source. Stakeholder trust is increased by this degree of transparency, which also makes it possible to quickly pinpoint the cause of any problems or delays.

Smart contracts, or self-executing contracts with predetermined terms and conditions, can be implemented thanks to blockchain technology. Aspects of supply chain activities including order fulfillment, payment processing, and quality control are all automated via smart contracts. Through the elimination of middlemen and manual procedures, smart contracts improve productivity and lower overhead. Blockchain's decentralized structure helps guarantee that information is safe from alteration and unwanted access. Since every block is cryptographically connected to the one before it, past transactions can seldom be changed without the network's collective consent. By ensuring the security and integrity of supply chain data, this feature lowers the possibility of fraud and data breaches.

Increased product authentication and traceability are two of the main benefits of implementing blockchain in supply chain management. Blockchain provides end-to-end traceability of products, enabling businesses and consumers to track the origin, manufacturing process, and transportation of goods. This feature is especially valuable in industries with complex supply chains, such as food and pharmaceuticals, where product authentication and provenance are critical for ensuring product quality and safety. Additionally, blockchain's transparent and auditable nature fosters trust among supply chain participants. Each stakeholder can access real-time data on the movement of goods, ensuring accountability and minimizing the risk of fraud or discrepancies in inventory records. Furthermore, blockchain enables businesses to optimize inventory management by providing a real-time visibility into inventory levels and product movement. Improved inventory tracking and forecasting lead to reduced carrying costs and stockouts, enhancing overall supply chain efficiency. Moreover, blockchain's ability to authenticate products and record every transaction in the supply chain helps detect and prevent counterfeit goods' distribution.

One of the primary challenges of blockchain implementation in supply chain management is scalability. Processing speeds on the blockchain network may get slower as the volume of transactions rises. Solutions like sharding and off-chain processing are being explored to address scalability issues. Integrating blockchain with existing supply chain systems and technologies can be complex. Hybrid solutions that combine blockchain with traditional databases are often used to facilitate a seamless transition. Data privacy and regulatory compliance are also critical concerns in blockchain adoption. Blockchain's transparency can raise concerns regarding data privacy and compliance with data protection regulations, such as the General Data Protection Regulation of the European Union. Businesses must ensure that sensitive data is appropriately encrypted and accessible only to authorized parties.

In the food and agriculture industry, blockchain technology is transforming food supply chains by enabling traceability from farm to fork. Through blockchain-based platforms, consumers can access information about food products' origin, production methods, and safety, promoting transparency and consumer confidence. In the pharmaceutical industry, blockchain is being utilized to trace the movement of drugs and medical supplies to prevent the circulation of counterfeit medications. This improves drug safety and streamlines regulatory compliance. Luxury brands leverage blockchain to verify the authenticity of high-value products, such as luxury watches and handbags. These brands protect their intellectual property and build customer trust by creating a digital certificate of authenticity on the blockchain.

Blockchain facilitates the creation of collaborative supply chain networks where all participants share real-time data securely. Better planning, coordination, and quicker reaction times to shifts in supply and demand are made possible by this.

To achieve widespread adoption, blockchain networks must be interoperable, allowing seamless communication and data sharing between different blockchain platforms. Standardization efforts are underway to address this challenge. Clear and consistent regulatory frameworks are essential for fostering blockchain adoption in supply chain management. For blockchain transactions to be considered legally valid and for blockchain records to be accepted in official documentation, governments and regulatory agencies must offer guidelines. Encouraging supply chain stakeholders to learn about and become aware of blockchain technology is essential to accelerating its adoption. In order to make an informed decision about implementing blockchain technology, businesses must be aware of its advantages and disadvantages.

Supply chain management is undergoing a radical change due to blockchain technology, which is transforming the ways that goods are tracked, verified, and delivered to customers. The enhanced traceability, transparency, and data security offered by blockchain contribute to improved efficiency, reduced costs, and increased consumer trust in supply chain operations. Despite scalability, integration, and regulatory compliance challenges, the potential benefits of blockchain adoption in supply chain management make it a compelling investment for businesses seeking to optimize their global trade and logistics processes. As industry-specific applications continue to evolve and collaborative supply chain networks gain momentum, blockchain's impact on supply chain management is poised to reshape the future of global commerce, creating a more transparent, efficient, and resilient supply chain ecosystem.

Cryptocurrency Adoption in Developing Countries

Cryptocurrencies, the digital assets powered by blockchain technology, have garnered significant attention worldwide, but their impact is particularly pronounced in developing countries. These nations, characterized by limited access to traditional financial services and unstable economies, have embraced cryptocurrencies as a means to foster financial inclusion, empower individuals with economic autonomy, and drive economic growth. In this section, we will explore the reasons behind the rising cryptocurrency adoption in developing countries, the advantages it brings to the underbanked and unbanked populations, and the challenges and opportunities that lie ahead in this transformative journey.

In many developing countries, a considerable portion of the population lacks access to fundamental financial services, such as banking accounts and credit facilities. Traditional banking systems often have limited reach, especially in rural areas, leaving many individuals excluded from the formal financial system. Moreover, high transaction costs associated with traditional remittance methods, such as money transfer operators, can diminish the value of remittances received by recipients. Additionally, developing countries are often prone to currency instability and high inflation rates, eroding the local currency's purchasing power. Citizens may seek refuge in more stable assets to protect their savings from devaluation.

Cryptocurrencies offer the unbanked and underbanked populations an opportunity to access financial services without a traditional banking infrastructure. Through a smartphone and internet connection, individuals can participate in the global economy, conduct transactions, and store value securely. Cryptocurrency transactions often involve lower fees than traditional banking systems, making them an attractive alternative for remittances. Peer-to-peer cryptocurrency transfers can bypass intermediaries, facilitating faster and more cost-effective cross-border remittances. Moreover, cryptocurrencies can act as a hedge against local currency devaluation and inflation. By holding digital assets, individuals can preserve the value of their wealth in times of economic uncertainty. Furthermore, cryptocurrencies open up investment opportunities beyond traditional asset classes for individuals in developing countries. They can invest in digital assets, participate in initial coin offerings (ICOs), and engage in decentralized finance (DeFi) protocols, potentially generating higher returns.

Promoting financial education and awareness about cryptocurrencies is crucial in encouraging adoption. Governments, non-governmental organizations (NGOs), and private institutions can collaborate to provide educational resources and workshops on cryptocurrency basics and safe practices. Mobile phones are more prevalent in many developing countries than traditional banking services. Developing user-friendly mobile applications that enable cryptocurrency transactions can facilitate adoption among the tech-savvy population. Clear and appropriate regulatory frameworks are essential to provide legal certainty and consumer protection in cryptocurrency transactions. Developing countries should work to strike a balance between fostering innovation and mitigating potential risks associated with digital assets.

In some rural areas of developing countries, access to reliable internet connectivity may be limited, hindering the widespread adoption of cryptocurrencies. Governments and private sector entities must invest in improving digital infrastructure to facilitate cryptocurrency usage. Cryptocurrencies are well-known for their price volatility, which can pose risks to individuals with limited financial literacy. Educating users about the risks and potential rewards of investing in digital assets is crucial to avoid undue financial losses. The lack of consumer protection and regulatory oversight in some developing countries can expose users to fraudulent schemes and scams related to cryptocurrencies. Efforts to raise awareness about potential scams and encourage responsible investing are vital.

Venezuela has experienced hyperinflation and economic instability, leading to widespread cryptocurrency adoption. Citizens turn to cryptocurrencies like Bitcoin as a store of value to protect their savings from the rapid devaluation of the local currency. In Nigeria, a large portion of the population is unbanked, and remittances play a significant role in the economy. The adoption of cryptocurrencies like Ethereum and Bitcoin has grown as individuals seek faster and cheaper remittance options.

Cryptocurrency adoption has the potential to drive economic growth in developing countries by empowering individuals with financial inclusion. Increased access to financial services and investment opportunities can spur entrepreneurial activity and foster economic development. Moreover, cryptocurrencies can facilitate cross-border trade by providing a seamless and cost-effective payment mechanism. This can enhance international trade relationships and promote economic cooperation between developing nations. Developing countries may gradually shift away from traditional banking systems as cryptocurrency adoption grows.

Digital assets can be a viable alternative for financial transactions and asset preservation.

Cryptocurrency adoption in developing countries has the potential to reshape financial landscapes and empower individuals with economic autonomy. By fostering financial inclusion, reducing transaction costs, and providing a hedge against currency instability, cryptocurrencies offer new opportunities for economic growth and prosperity. To harness the full potential of digital assets, stakeholders must work together to address infrastructure, regulation, and financial literacy challenges. As more developing nations embrace cryptocurrencies, the transformative impact on their economies and the lives of their citizens will become increasingly evident, ushering in a new era of financial empowerment and economic resilience.

CHAPTER X

Challenges and Future Outlook

Scalability and Energy Concerns

A new era of digital commerce and decentralized finance has been brought about by cryptocurrencies. However, the difficulties associated with scalability and energy consumption also increase with the growing popularity of cryptocurrencies. The capacity of a blockchain network to manage a growing volume of transactions effectively is known as scalability, whereas energy concerns are related to the effects that cryptocurrency mining operations have on the environment. This section will examine the complexities of energy and scalability challenges surrounding cryptocurrencies, as well as the many strategies used by blockchain projects to balance innovation and sustainability.

The scalability challenge in cryptocurrencies is rooted in what is commonly known as the "trilemma." Achieving scalability, security, and decentralization simultaneously is a complex task. While a centralized system can achieve high scalability at the cost of decentralization and security, a fully decentralized network may sacrifice scalability to maintain security and decentralization. Striking the right balance among these three aspects is a significant challenge for blockchain developers. The demand on a blockchain network's ability to process transactions fast grows with the amount of users and transactions on it. The usefulness of cryptocurrencies for regular transactions can be limited by lengthy confirmation periods and expensive transaction fees, which can negatively impact the user experience. Bitcoin and Ethereum, as two of the most prominent cryptocurrencies, have faced scalability challenges due to their design. Bitcoin's block time of 10 minutes and Ethereum's 15-second block time contribute to slower transaction processing. Both networks have experienced congestion during peak usage periods, leading to delays and higher fees.

Various solutions have been proposed and implemented to address scalability challenges in the cryptocurrency space. Off-chain scaling solutions aim to reduce the burden on the main blockchain by conducting some transactions off-chain. One example is the Lightning Network for Bitcoin, which enables fast and low-cost transactions by creating user payment channels. In order to enable quicker and more scalable transactions, Layer 2 solutions are constructed on top of existing blockchains. Projects like Ethereum's "Ethereum 2.0" and "Polygon" aim to address Ethereum's scalability issues through sharding and side chains. Additionally, interoperability between different blockchains can also enhance scalability. Projects like Polkadot and Cosmos focus on enabling communication and transactions between multiple blockchains, expanding the overall capacity of the ecosystem.

The energy concerns in cryptocurrency primarily revolve around the energy-intensive nature of Proof-of-Work (PoW) consensus mechanisms used by some blockchains. In order to confirm transactions and add blocks to the blockchain using Proof of Work (PoW), miners must compete by solving intricate mathematical puzzles, which demands a significant amount of computational power. This process demands significant energy resources and results in high electricity consumption. The energy consumption of PoW-based cryptocurrencies has drawn criticism for its environmental impact, as mining operations often rely on fossil fuels and contribute to carbon emissions. Critics argue that the carbon footprint of cryptocurrencies poses challenges to global sustainability efforts.

Some blockchain projects are transitioning from PoW to Proof-of-Stake (PoS) consensus mechanisms to address energy concerns. PoS does not require resource-intensive mining but instead relies on validators who are chosen to create blocks based on the amount of cryptocurrency they "stake" or lock up as collateral. This shift to PoS reduces the energy consumption associated with mining. In an effort to mitigate their carbon footprint, mining companies are also looking into more energy-efficient techniques like employing renewable energy sources. Initiatives like the Crypto Climate Accord aim to make the cryptocurrency industry 100% renewable by 2025.
To be a competitive alternative to established financial systems, cryptocurrencies must be innovative and scalable in order to be widely adopted. Faster and cheaper transactions are critical for encouraging everyday use and facilitating global commerce. Innovations in blockchain technology are necessary to overcome the scalability challenges while maintaining security and decentralization. However, the cryptocurrency community must also embrace sustainable mining and network operation practices to address energy concerns. Transitioning to PoS and exploring renewable energy sources can significantly reduce the environmental impact of cryptocurrencies.

Collaboration among blockchain projects, researchers, and environmentalists is vital to develop sustainable solutions for the industry. Research into energy-efficient consensus mechanisms and eco-friendly mining practices can pave the way for a greener cryptocurrency ecosystem. Moreover, governments and regulatory bodies can play a role in promoting sustainability in the cryptocurrency industry. Positive change can be sparked by incentives and regulations that support the utilization of renewable energy sources in mining. Through collaborative efforts among stakeholders, the cryptocurrency community can pave the way for a more scalable, energy-efficient, and sustainable future, positioning digital assets as a transformative force in the global economy.

Scalability and energy concerns are critical challenges that the cryptocurrency industry must address to ensure its continued growth and sustainability. Finding solutions that balance innovation with environmental responsibility is key to securing the future of cryptocurrencies. Off-chain scaling solutions, layer 2 solutions, and interoperability can enhance scalability, making cryptocurrencies more practical for everyday use. Transitioning to PoS and adopting energy-efficient mining practices are crucial steps toward reducing the industry's environmental impact. Through collaborative efforts among stakeholders, the cryptocurrency community can pave the way for a more scalable, energy-efficient, and sustainable future, positioning digital assets as a transformative force in the global economy. As the industry continues to evolve, striking the right balance between innovation and sustainability will be essential to foster cryptocurrencies' widespread adoption and long-term viability in the modern financial landscape.

Potential Roadblocks to Cryptocurrency Adoption

The rise of cryptocurrencies has seen tremendous growth and innovation, promising decentralized finance and empowering individuals with financial autonomy. However, despite their potential, widespread adoption of cryptocurrencies faces several roadblocks that hinder their integration into mainstream financial systems. This section explores the potential challenges hindering cryptocurrency adoption, including regulatory complexities, technological limitations, security concerns, lack of consumer awareness, and resistance from traditional financial institutions. Understanding and addressing these roadblocks are crucial in devising strategies to pave the way for a more inclusive and robust cryptocurrency ecosystem.

The lack of clarity and uniformity in cryptocurrency regulations presents significant challenges to market participants. Different countries have varying approaches to cryptocurrency regulation, leading to uncertainty for businesses and consumers. Strict Anti-Money Laundering (AML) and Know Your Customer (KYC) compliance requirements may deter users who prioritize privacy. Moreover, navigating the complexities of cryptocurrency taxation and reporting can lead to user confusion and compliance issues.

Scalability remains a persistent challenge for blockchain networks, resulting in slow transaction processing and high fees during peak usage. The absence of interoperability between different blockchain networks hinders seamless communication and the transfer of assets, hindering cross-chain transactions. The user experience of interacting with cryptocurrencies can be daunting for non-technical users, requiring user-friendly interfaces and intuitive applications to enhance accessibility.

The cryptocurrency space has experienced several high-profile hacks and vulnerabilities, leading to significant user losses. Robust security measures are essential to protect user funds and instill trust in the cryptocurrency ecosystem. Additionally, phishing attacks and scams pose risks to unsuspecting users, necessitating awareness campaigns to safeguard them from fraudulent schemes.

Cryptocurrencies can appear complex and intimidating to newcomers, partially due to the use of technical jargon. Educating the general public about the basics of cryptocurrencies and their potential benefits is crucial in fostering adoption. Misinformation and fear, uncertainty, and doubt (FUD) propagated by various sources can mislead potential users, requiring accurate information dissemination to dispel myths and build trust.

Cryptocurrencies represent a disruptive force in the financial industry, challenging traditional banking and payment systems. Resistance from established financial institutions may hinder the integration of cryptocurrencies into mainstream financial services. Regulatory uncertainty and compliance risks may also contribute to the reluctance of traditional financial institutions to embrace cryptocurrencies fully.

To overcome these roadblocks, collaborative efforts are essential. Governments, regulatory bodies, and industry stakeholders must work together to develop clear and balanced regulatory frameworks. Blockchain projects should prioritize technological innovations addressing scalability, interoperability, and user experience challenges. Enhanced security measures in cryptocurrency exchanges and wallets can instill confidence among users. Educational initiatives should be intensified to raise awareness and inform the public about secure practices and responsible investing. Collaborating with traditional financial institutions through partnerships and pilot projects can demonstrate the benefits of integrating cryptocurrencies into existing financial services.

Cryptocurrencies have the capacity to transform the financial landscape, but several roadblocks hinder their mainstream adoption. Regulatory complexities, technological limitations, security concerns, lack of consumer awareness, and resistance from traditional financial institutions pose significant hurdles. Addressing these challenges requires collaborative efforts from governments, industry stakeholders, and the broader community. Clear and balanced regulatory frameworks, technological innovations, enhanced security measures, educational initiatives, and collaboration with traditional finance are essential in fostering the widespread adoption of cryptocurrencies. As the industry evolves, addressing these challenges will pave the way for a more inclusive, secure, and integrated cryptocurrency ecosystem, unlocking the full potential of digital assets in the modern financial landscape.

The Future of Cryptocurrencies

The rise of cryptocurrencies has seen a meteoric growth since the introduction of Bitcoin in 2009. Over the years, cryptocurrencies have captured the imagination of tech enthusiasts, investors, and even governments worldwide. As we look to the future, it is evident that cryptocurrencies will continue to shape the financial landscape, introducing transformative changes and challenging traditional financial systems. This section explores the potential of cryptocurrencies in reshaping the future of finance, the innovations driving their growth, the challenges they must overcome, and the potential impact on global economies.

The invention of Bitcoin by an unidentified individual or group known only as Satoshi Nakamoto marked the beginning of the cryptocurrency adventure. Over time, Bitcoin paved the way for a new era of digital currencies, commonly referred to as "altcoins." Ethereum emerged as a groundbreaking platform that introduced smart contracts, enabling programmable transactions and decentralized applications (dApps). The creation of various altcoins diversified the cryptocurrency landscape, each with unique features and use cases. Moreover, the rise of decentralized finance (DeFi) projects leverages blockchain technology to offer a range of financial services without intermediaries, such as lending, borrowing, and yield farming. DeFi has the potential to democratize financial access and eliminate traditional gatekeepers, enabling users to participate in financial activities directly. Additionally, central banks worldwide have started exploring the concept of central bank digital currencies (CBDCs), digital representations of fiat currencies that aim to offer the benefits of cryptocurrencies while maintaining regulatory oversight and stability. CBDCs could potentially revolutionize cross- border payments and financial transactions.

Blockchain technology, the backbone of cryptocurrencies, continues to evolve. Improvements in scalability, consensus mechanisms, and interoperability are being explored to address the challenges of handling large transaction volumes and enabling seamless communication between different blockchain networks. NFTs (non-fungible tokens) have emerged as a groundbreaking application of blockchain technology, enabling the creation and trading of unique digital assets. NFTs have found applications in art, gaming, collectibles, and more, transforming the concept of digital ownership and intellectual property rights. Furthermore, interoperability solutions are being developed to enable communication between different blockchain networks, fostering a more interconnected cryptocurrency ecosystem. Projects like Polkadot and Cosmos are pioneering cross-chain communication, transferring assets seamlessly between diverse blockchains.

The regulatory environment surrounding cryptocurrencies remains complex and varies from country to country. Balancing fostering innovation and protecting consumers and investors is a significant challenge. Clarity and uniformity in regulations are essential to provide a conducive environment for cryptocurrency growth. Security remains a critical concern in the cryptocurrency space. Cyberattacks, hacks, and scams pose risks to users and the industry as a whole. Privacy concerns have also come to the forefront, prompting discussions about the need for privacy-enhancing technologies while addressing potential illicit activities. Moreover, some cryptocurrencies use Proof-of-Work (PoW) consensus mechanisms are energy-intensive and have raised environmental concerns. Transitioning to more energy-efficient consensus mechanisms like Proof-of-Stake (PoS) and exploring renewable energy solutions are vital for ensuring the sustainability of cryptocurrencies.

Because they give underbanked and unbanked people access to financial services, cryptocurrencies have the possibility to promote financial inclusion. DeFi projects can offer loans and savings opportunities to individuals without the need for traditional banks. Cross-border payments facilitated by cryptocurrencies can significantly reduce transaction fees and processing times, benefiting individuals and businesses engaged in international trade. The rise of private cryptocurrencies and CBDCs raises questions about the role of traditional sovereign currencies in the future financial landscape. Central banks must adapt to the changing dynamics of digital currencies while maintaining monetary stability.

Collaboration between governments, regulatory bodies, and the cryptocurrency industry is crucial in developing clear and balanced regulatory frameworks. Emphasizing consumer protection, security, and privacy while encouraging innovation can promote responsible growth. Education is vital in fostering adoption and dispelling misconceptions about cryptocurrencies. Initiatives to promote financial literacy and responsible investing can empower individuals to make informed decisions. Sustainability efforts, such as transitioning to energy-efficient consensus mechanisms and promoting eco-friendly mining practices, are essential to address environmental concerns. Embracing technological innovations will drive the continued evolution of cryptocurrencies and their applications.

The future of cryptocurrencies promises a decentralized and transformative financial landscape. As the industry evolves, innovations like DeFi, NFTs, and CBDCs will continue to reshape how we interact with money and assets. Challenges, such as regulatory complexities, security concerns, and environmental impacts, must be addressed collaboratively. The potential impact of cryptocurrencies on global economies, financial inclusion, and cross-border transactions is significant. Through responsible regulation, education, and technological advancements, cryptocurrencies are poised to usher in a new era of financial empowerment, democratization, and economic growth. Embracing the potential of cryptocurrencies with a forward-looking and balanced approach will be key in unlocking the full benefits of this revolutionary technology in the years to come.

CONCLUSION

Recap of Key Points

Throughout this extensive exploration of cryptocurrencies, we have delved into various aspects of this transformative digital asset class. Cryptocurrencies have left an indelible mark on the global financial landscape, from their inception with Bitcoin to the rise of altcoins, decentralized finance (DeFi), and central bank digital currencies (CBDCs). This recap will summarize the key points discussed, providing a comprehensive overview of the cryptocurrency journey.

The cryptocurrency journey began with the creation of Bitcoin in 2009 by the enigmatic figure known as Satoshi Nakamoto. Bitcoin pioneered a decentralized financial system, introducing the concept of blockchain technology and digital scarcity through its limited supply of 21 million coins. This revolutionary idea of a trustless, peer-to-peer electronic cash system sparked the cryptocurrency revolution. As Bitcoin gained prominence, it paved the way for the emergence of alternative cryptocurrencies with their unique features and use cases. Ethereum, with its smart contract capabilities, revolutionized the landscape by enabling the development of decentralized applications and ushering in the era of DeFi.

Cryptocurrencies have witnessed remarkable innovations that have contributed to their growth and adoption. Non-fungible tokens (NFTs) introduced a novel concept of digital ownership, enabling the creation and trading of unique digital assets. The creation of NFTs has found applications in various industries, from art and music to gaming and virtual real estate. Moreover, DeFi has emerged as a game-changer, offering various financial services without intermediaries. Decentralized exchanges, lending platforms, and yield farming have flourished within the DeFi space, enabling users to access financial services directly, irrespective of their geographical location or traditional banking status.

Despite their potential, cryptocurrencies face several challenges that must be addressed for widespread adoption. Regulatory complexities vary from country to country, creating uncertainty for businesses and consumers alike. Balancing fostering innovation and protecting consumers is crucial for the sustainable growth of the cryptocurrency industry. Security concerns, including cyberattacks and scams, pose user risks and undermine the ecosystem's confidence. Privacy-enhancing technologies and robust security measures are essential to safeguard users' funds and data. Furthermore, the environmental impact of energy-intensive mining operations has led to discussions on transitioning to more energy-efficient consensus mechanisms and promoting renewable energy sources within the industry.

Cryptocurrencies have a great deal of potential to promote financial inclusion by giving underbanked and unbanked people access to financial services. Individuals without access to regular banking services might benefit from DeFi projects by being able to apply for loans and save money. Moreover, cross-border payments facilitated by cryptocurrencies can significantly reduce transaction fees and processing times, benefiting individuals and businesses engaged in international trade. The rise of CBDCs marks a new chapter in the financial landscape, with central banks exploring the concept of issuing digital representations of fiat currencies. CBDCs could streamline cross-border transactions, enhance financial transparency, and improve monetary policy management.

The future of cryptocurrencies lies in fostering collaboration between governments, regulatory bodies, and industry stakeholders. Clear and balanced regulatory frameworks that emphasize consumer protection and security will create a conducive environment for cryptocurrency growth. Education and awareness initiatives are vital to dispel misconceptions and encourage responsible investing in cryptocurrencies. Sustainability efforts, such as transitioning to eco-friendly mining practices and energy-efficient consensus mechanisms, will address environmental concerns and pave the way for a greener cryptocurrency ecosystem. Embracing technological innovations will drive the continuous evolution of cryptocurrencies and their potential applications, unlocking their full benefits for users worldwide.

The cryptocurrency journey has been a rollercoaster of innovation, challenges, and opportunities. From the humble beginnings of Bitcoin to the diverse landscape of altcoins and DeFi, cryptocurrencies have disrupted traditional finance and offered a glimpse of a decentralized future. Innovations like NFTs and DeFi have redefined digital ownership and financial services, empowering users with greater control over their assets and financial decisions. Nevertheless, the path forward requires collaboration, education, and sustainable practices to address regulatory complexities, security concerns, and environmental impacts. By striking the right balance and embracing innovation responsibly, cryptocurrencies can pave the way for a more inclusive, transparent, and decentralized financial landscape, shaping the future of finance for generations to come.

Encouragement for Readers to Embrace Cryptocurrencies

In the fast-paced world of technological advancements, cryptocurrencies have emerged as a groundbreaking financial innovation that promises to transform how we interact with money and assets. While cryptocurrencies have been met with enthusiasm and skepticism, their potential for empowering individuals, fostering financial inclusion, and challenging traditional financial systems cannot be ignored. This section aims to encourage readers to embrace cryptocurrencies by exploring their benefits, debunking common misconceptions, and providing practical tips for adopting responsible cryptocurrency.

At the core of cryptocurrencies lies the concept of financial empowerment, offering individuals greater control over their financial assets and decisions. Traditional financial systems often involve intermediaries such as banks and payment processors, adding complexities and fees to transactions. Cryptocurrencies enable direct peer-to-peer transactions, eliminating the need for intermediaries and reducing transaction costs. This newfound financial autonomy empowers individuals to transact freely, irrespective of geographical boundaries, and gain access to a global financial network.

Cryptocurrencies can potentially bridge the gap between the banked and unbanked populations. Approximately 1.7 billion of individuals worldwide lack access to traditional banking services, hindering their participation in the global economy. Cryptocurrencies offer an opportunity for financial inclusion by providing access to financial services through the internet and a smartphone. Empowering the unbanked with the ability to send and receive money, access loans, and engage in financial activities can have a transformative impact on their lives and livelihoods.

Despite the numerous benefits, cryptocurrencies have faced skepticism and misconceptions. Concerns about security, volatility, and association with illicit activities have often been raised. It is necessary to dispel these myths and educate the public about the fundamentals of cryptocurrencies. While security measures are imperative, many cryptocurrencies leverage advanced cryptographic principles to ensure robust security. Volatility, while inherent in some cryptocurrencies, is a characteristic that may diminish with increased adoption and market maturity. Moreover, cryptocurrencies are not solely associated with illicit activities, as they have a wide range of legitimate use cases, including cross-border remittances, smart contracts, and decentralized applications.

Embracing cryptocurrencies entails a responsible approach to investing and transacting. As with any financial asset, risks are involved, and individuals must exercise due diligence and only invest what they can afford to lose. Diversifying one's investment portfolio and avoiding FOMO (Fear of Missing Out) are prudent strategies to mitigate risk. Additionally, individuals should educate themselves about secure practices, such as storing cryptocurrencies in reputable wallets and enabling two-factor authentication. The cryptocurrency space offers many resources for learning and connecting with experienced individuals, making it accessible to newcomers.

One concern often raised is the environmental impact of cryptocurrency mining, particularly in proof-of-work (PoW) networks. However, the industry is actively exploring more energy-efficient consensus mechanisms like proof-of-stake (PoS) and sustainable mining practices. Transitioning to eco-friendly alternatives is essential for ensuring the long-term sustainability of cryptocurrencies while mitigating environmental concerns.

Cryptocurrencies represent the vanguard of a new era of finance that challenges the dominance of traditional financial institutions and central authorities. The rise of decentralized finance (DeFi) and the exploration of central bank digital currencies (CBDCs) signal a paradigm shift in the financial landscape. Embracing cryptocurrencies is an opportunity to be part of this transformative journey, shaping the future of finance by contributing to an inclusive, transparent, and decentralized financial system.

Cryptocurrencies offer an unprecedented opportunity for financial empowerment and inclusivity, empowering individuals with greater control over their financial assets and decisions. Debunking misconceptions, educating the public, and adopting responsible practices are crucial in fostering the widespread adoption of cryptocurrencies. Embracing cryptocurrencies has the potential to reshape the global financial landscape and offers individuals a means to take charge of their financial future. By embracing this financial revolution, readers can help create a financial system that is more accessible and equitable while also enabling future generations to realize the immense potential of cryptocurrencies.

Thank you for buying and reading/ listening to our book. If you found this book useful/ helpful please take a few minutes and leave a review on the platform where you purchased our book. Your feedback matters greatly to us.

www.ingramcontent.com/pod-product-compliance
Lightning Source LLC
Chambersburg PA
CBHW071320130726
47996CB00002B/553